IF MY PEOPLE

Exploring our Partnership with God

*"If my people, who are called by my name,
will humble themselves and pray and seek my face
and turn from their wicked ways, then will I hear
from heaven and will forgive their sin
and will heal their land."*

(2 Chronicles 7:14)

ROBERT GRIFFITH

GRACE AND TRUTH PUBLISHING
PO Box 338, Gunnedah NSW 2380 Australia
www.graceandtruthpublishing.com.au

All Bible quotes are from the New International Version (NIV) expect where otherwise stated.

NEW INTERNATIONAL VERSION (NIV), Copyright 1973, 1978 and 1984 by international Bible Society. Used by permission of Zondervan Publishing House. All rights reserved.

Other version quotes are from:

AMPLIFIED BIBLE (AMP), Copyright © 1954, 1958, 1962, 1964, 1965, 1987 by The Lockman Foundation. Used by permission.

ENGLISH STANDARD VERSION (ESV), Copyright © 2001 by Crossway Bibles, a division of Good News Publishers. Used by permission. All rights reserved.

NEW AMERICAN STANDARD BIBLE (NASB), Copyright © 1960, 1962, 1963, 1968, 1971, 1972, 1973, 1975, 1977, by The Lockman Foundation. Used by permission.

NEW KING JAMES VERSION (NKJV), Copyright © 1979, 1980, 1982, by Thomas Nelson Inc. Used by permission. All rights reserved.

THE MESSAGE (MSG), by Eugene Peterson, Copyright © 1993, 1994, 1995, 1996, and 2000. Used by permission of NavPress Publishing Group. All rights reserved.

REVISED STANDARD VERSION (RSV), Copyright © 1973, by Thomas Nelson Inc. Used by permission. All rights reserved.

ISBN 978-0-6486439-8-2

TABLE OF CONTENTS

PREFACE

In my first book, *Amazing Grace,* I went to considerable lengths to establish the foundation of our entire Christian experience. That foundation is grace, and everything must be built upon that sure footing. Grace is not just one of many beliefs or doctrines we need to embrace. Grace is not *part of* the gospel; grace *is* the gospel, and the gospel *is* grace! In fact, grace is to the Christian faith what oxygen is to us all. If we do not have a firm grasp of grace; if grace has not had its effect within us, then all we have is a facade, a shell, a pseudo-Christian 'religion' with no power, motivation, or the ability to fulfil our true purpose as God's children. Unless we have a firm understanding of God's amazing grace; unless His grace permeates everything that we think, say, and do every day, then our Christian lives will lack substance, vitality, and power.

I want you to imagine the above truths about grace forming one of two railway tracks upon which our 'train' runs. Two tracks are needed, and they must be exactly parallel, and they are equal in their importance. You can't have one without the other. You cannot favour one over the other. You cannot set them against each other. Our whole train will derail, and our journey will come to an abrupt and fruitless end unless both tracks are firmly in place and never moved.

With that analogy in mind, I want to suggest that this book has been written to help us understand the other railway track. The first track is all about God and what He has done and continues to do through His grace, His empowering presence. The second track is all about us and what we have been called to do and who we have been called to be, in partnership with God.

Looking back over my forty plus years as a preacher and teacher, I could safely say that the main thrust of all my preaching could be found within these two books. I think *Amazing Grace* and *If My People* are foundational to everything I believe, and all that God wants us to embrace. Questions which may come to mind when reading *Amazing Grace* are answered in this book and questions which may arise from this book are answered in *Amazing Grace.*

Now at your first glance, it may appear that I have written 225 pages about just one verse in the Bible! Not even someone as verbose as me could achieve such an epic feat. Nor would I think it was appropriate to use 2 Chronicles 7:14 as a verse to directly apply to our current situation. It is important that my readers understand what I am <u>not</u> doing here.

The promise of God which is contained in 2 Chronicles 7:14 has an original context which can and should never be overridden or lost when we read it and understand it today. Many preachers have lifted this specific verse out of its context and applied it directly to the modern era. That is never appropriate, and I am not suggesting that this specific promise was given by God to every person in every 'land' for all time, not directly, anyway.

However, if you were to come after me with the charge that this verse does not apply to us today, you would be right *and* you would also be wrong. You would be right for the reason I have outlined above. The specific application of the truths within this verse belong to and apply to the people of God at a specific time and location in history. However, the foundational principles and truths contained within this amazing verse, reveal God's heart for <u>all</u> His people, in <u>every</u> age and <u>every</u> situation.

I am very comfortable using this amazing verse as a springboard to many other parts of the Bible which are universally applicable and speak to every generation. Understanding who 'My people' are; learning about humility, prayer, intimacy with God; sin and repentance; gaining a firm understanding of God's deep desire to bring healing to every land at every point in history . . . those are universal truths and essential aspects of our faith journey.

So, if you ask me if God directed 2 Chronicles 7:14 to us in our current context, I would say 'no.' If you ask me if God *could have* said the same words to us in our context and been true to the revelation of Scripture, then I would answer with a resounding 'yes.' So, let's build that second railway track, shall we?

Robert Griffith

CHAPTER ONE
A Hard Word

I have a passion for the grace of God. Grace lies at the heart of the gospel of Jesus Christ. I have preached the grace of God over and over again for decades now. I have stood at the gates of Hell and preached the grace of God in the face of the enemy as He attacked me and my family and my congregation and my city in multiple locations over forty years.

The grace of God is the key to life. The grace of God is the foundation of the Christian faith. The grace of God reveals the essence of God in His dealings with us and so I gladly join the Apostle Paul in saying, *"By the grace of God I am what I am .."* I can also say that by the grace of God you are what you are and by the grace of God, the church is what it is today. But there was another important part of that statement from Paul – let's read it.

> *"By the grace of God I am what I am, and his grace to me was not without effect. No, I worked harder than all of them - yet not I, but the grace of God that was with me." (1 Corinthians 15:10)*

This verse is therefore just like a two-sided coin – it contains two distinct but equally important truths:

By the grace of God I am what I am

His grace to me was not without effect

So, what *effect* has the grace of God had in you and through you? Has your knowledge of God's amazing grace changed your understanding of God and yourself and sin and forgiveness? Has grace changed the way you think about all sorts of things? What effect has God's grace had in your life and ministry?

You may be able to affirm that you rejoice in the knowledge of the grace of God, and you know that you are saved by His grace and that even your best efforts are filthy rags in His sight and affirm all that you are and ever hope to be, has its beginning and end in the grace of God.

You may affirm that your life will never be the same because you understand God's grace. Many believers can't even say that, but perhaps you can. I certainly hope and pray that anyone who has engaged with my teaching for any length of time has a deeper and broader understanding of God's amazing grace.

However, what do you say when I flip the coin and ask what *effect* has God's grace had in your life? How are you living in response to the revelation of God's amazing grace? It is great for us to focus on God's grace and all the hard work He has done in Christ to secure our salvation and bless us with every spiritual blessing, but there comes a time when we need to ask what our role is in all of this in terms of *our response* to His grace.

All through the Bible, God reminds us of the need for us to respond in certain ways if His grace is to have any real effect in saving this lost world. The strongest and clearest reminder of our role in all this is contained in one verse from the Old Testament which will form the framework for all that I share in this book:

> *"If my people, who are called by my name, will humble themselves and pray and seek my face and turn from their wicked ways, then will I hear from heaven and will forgive their sin and will heal their land." (2 Chronicles 7:14)*

Allow me to paraphrase that to make it even clearer:

> *"If my people … who understand My grace and have been blessed by the revelation of Who I am … if My people live out of the reality of that grace … in humility, brokenness, worship, confession, and prayer … then that grace will not be without effect … I will heal their entire land … through them."*

As I began to lay out the framework for this book, I found myself reflecting on the thousands of hours that I have stood before God's people and poured out my heart, doing everything I can to connect people with God's heart. It has been a joy to journey with hundreds of brothers and sisters in Christ within various congregations over many years and serve them by expounding God's Word.

In recent years it has been a new experience and a really great encouragement to be able to also use the internet to spread my teaching across the whole world.

However, I must be honest and confess that there are also times when I ponder how ineffective most of that teaching has been in producing long-term, life-changing responses in people. I am reminded often that the Apostle Paul referred to this thing that I do every week as *foolishness*. To pour one's heart and soul into sermons week after week after week, year after year after year, must seem like foolishness to any rational, thinking person. And yet, God's call to preach and teach has never been stronger in me. There are however, many times when I find myself reflecting on these confronting words:

> *"We have much to say about this, but it is hard to explain because you are slow to learn. In fact, though by this time you ought to be teachers, you need someone to teach you the elementary truths of God's word all over again. You need milk, not solid food! Anyone who lives on milk, being still an infant, is not acquainted with the teaching about righteousness. But solid food is for the mature, who by constant use have trained themselves to distinguish good from evil. Therefore, let us leave the elementary teachings about Christ and go on to maturity, not laying again the foundation … and God permitting, we will do so." (Hebrews 5:11-6:3)*

Where is the hunger and thirst for righteousness? Where is the passion and longing in people's hearts to hear from God? Where is the ache deep within us for our city and our nation, such that we will do anything to gain an edge on the enemy and make a difference in our community?

Where are the people of God who know that they have been bought with a price and have a call on their life to shine as lights in the darkness and that this call of God is the most important thing in their life - above their family, their job, their worldly success and even their very lives?

I warned you in the title of this opening chapter that this was 'a hard word.' Which reminds of this interaction between Jesus and His disciples all those years ago:

> *"Many of Jesus' disciples said, "This is a hard teaching. Who can accept it?" ... Jesus said to them, "Does this offend you? ... The Spirit gives life; the flesh counts for nothing. The words I have spoken to you are spirit and they are life. Yet there are some of you who do not believe." ... From this time many of his disciples turned back and no longer followed him. "You do not want to leave too, do you?" Jesus asked the Twelve. (John 6:60-67)*

This is a hard word – but it's a really important word. Where are the people who are genuinely sick of playing Church; those who know there is more to the Christian life than they've experienced; those who now choose to do whatever it takes to see their lives, their Church fellowship and their city transformed and Jesus Christ reign as King and Lord?

Where are those people? The Bible calls them disciples. Are you one of them? Are there many in my city and yours? They are the ones who arrive early for worship services ... because they know that being with the people of God, in the presence of God, with the Word of God is the most exciting and life-changing activity in their whole week and they can't wait to be there, and they don't want to leave when it's over! Is that you?

I'm taking about the people who hang off every word preached; they take notes, they have their Bible's with them when someone is preaching so they can find the passages themselves and help reinforce all that God is saying to them; they are the ones who set aside time during the week to read the sermons online or watch the video or listen to the podcast so they can distil every gem of wisdom from God.

I'm looking for the ones who weep when they read or watch the news and see the needs in their city and nation which confront us all every day and which only God can fix - if and when His people stop pursuing their own selfish interests and really start focusing on the needs of those they are called to reach.

Where are those people? The committed, determined, focussed, maturing disciples; the ones who read the New Testament and take it seriously; the ones who have more interest in living in the book of Acts than in the materialistic, self-seeking, flesh-serving, Spirit-quenching world around them; the ones who have given up talking about themselves and their needs and their problems and their achievements and are now only interested in the needs of others and the furthering of God's Kingdom. Where are those people? Are you one of them? If not, then read on and see what God has in store for you!

What is the secret to being a full-on, committed, dynamic, world-changing disciple of Jesus Christ? What button do you push to make this all happen? Do you really want to know? You may not realise this but there is a simple answer to this question. There is, in fact, one button and only one button that you need to push to make all this happen. Do you want to know what that is? It's hard to miss below in your peripheral vision! This is the key to life; this is the button you push to catapult you into the reality the power, the glory, and the effectiveness of the Kingdom of God. There is just one simple word on that button.

CHOICE

Disappointed? Feeling conned? Perhaps you thought it would be something more 'spiritual.' Sorry about that. This button has been the catalyst for every major move of God, every revival and community transformation ever recorded in the whole history of mankind. Do you want to be a committed, effective passionate disciple of Jesus Christ?

That can and will happen ... but you have a choice to make first.

Do you want to move on from drinking the spiritual milk that has dominated the teaching of most Churches for years and get your teeth into a juicy piece of Kingdom Steak ... which will produce the kind of life-changing ministry in and through you that we read about in the Gospels and the book of Acts? Is that what you want?

That can and will happen ... but you have a choice to make first.

Do you want to see the Church emerge from the ashes of denominationalism, division, and dissention?

That can and will happen ... but you have a choice to make first.

Do you want to see the day when the Mayor of our City addresses an all-night prayer vigil and declares to the 10,000 people present that this city belongs to Jesus Christ?

That can and will happen ... but you have a choice to make first.

Do you want to see the day when everyone in this nation who needs a job, has a job; where domestic violence and sexual abuse are rare occurrences, not hourly events; where pubs and clubs close their doors because people now have lives to live which mean something?

That can and will happen ... but you have a choice to make first.

Do you want to see a headline in the newspaper which reads, "No arrests again this month. Police numbers cut."

That can and will happen ... but you have a choice to make first.

Do you want to be able to pray *"Your kingdom come, your will be done in my community as it is in heaven"* and then see the reality of heaven unfold right before your eyes ... as the blind see, the deaf hear, the lame dance and the power and glory and majesty and love of God flood your entire city and nation?

That can and will happen ... but you have a choice to make first.

All these wild, pie-in-the-sky dreams I have laid out before you just now are already a reality for people just like you and me in hundreds of communities around the world.

Furthermore, all these crazy dreams just happen to be the plan and purpose and the expectation of God. Those wild ideas and unbelievable notions are actually what God desires for every one of us, every day of our lives. Do you know that? You don't need to ask His permission or seek His will on these things for they are clearly understood from the Bible and from all our human experience.

All that reality, all of those wonderful dreams of what might be, begin with you and me and people just like us all over the world, making a choice.

So, I can hear you ask, *"If it's that simple; if all we need to do is make a choice; why doesn't it happen every day? Why aren't those things a reality if simple choices are all that is needed?"* What great questions. I am so glad you asked!

I believe the reason is because something needs to happen <u>before</u> you can make that choice. Something vitally important has to be present in you in you if any choice is going to be effective. So many people have made a choice but ended up nowhere because they failed to have this one vital pre-requisite to all effective choices; what do you think that might be? The answer: **DESIRE.**

You have to get in touch with your deepest desires and decide what you <u>really</u> want in life. You have to decide what is really important to you - deep down inside. So many people make choices in life based on guilt or obligation; other people's needs or expectations; a sense of duty - all sorts of reasons.

Some of these reasons appear very noble and proper but I am here to tell you that if you don't <u>really</u> <u>desire</u> a particular thing; if you are not passionate about pursuing that goal until the very end; chances are very high that you won't ever get there.

Worse than that, making the choice to pursue that direction without the motivation and desire to follow through may well be the most frustrating, humiliating, depressing experience you ever have. So, please understand this:

There is no point making choices that are not consistent with your heart's desires.

It is a guaranteed recipe for disaster to make a choice in life, no matter how small or large, if that is not what you *really* want. That's why many marriages fail. That's why many Churches are ineffective. That's why many relationships fall apart.

We make choices which have not come from the depths of our heart's desire and therefore our ability to commit to those choices and pay the price to see them through to completion is radically reduced and more often than not, we will fail. This is a hard word, but I tell you that it may be the most important word you hear in your life, so stay with me here.

If you are not sure that you really want to be a disciple of Jesus then don't bother trying to make that happen, because it won't. If you are not gripped with a passion to see your community transformed spiritually, socially, economically, politically - in every possible way in fact - then don't bother praying for it; don't bother telling anyone about your passion to see your city come to Jesus, because you won't be part of any of it until you really <u>want</u> to be. Then, and only then, you must choose to pay the price to see that desire fulfilled.

If you are not committed to drawing as much as you can from the teaching you receive from me and all the other sources you access, it is simply because you don't want to; it's just not that important to you.

Now let me assure you that I don't want you to do anything you don't want to do. I will always defend your freedom in the grace of God to do whatever your heart desires.

If you want to sit in the corner and drool and waste your whole life while Satan kicks the stuffing out of thousands of people in the city you call home – that's your choice and I will love you no less for it. God will love you no less for it. You will just have wasted so much of your life in this world.

If, however, the Holy Spirit gets under your skin and releases a passion and hunger and desire within you for the Word of God; if there's this energy within you which draws you to solid Bible teaching and releases an insatiable desire in you for truth and wisdom and the heart and mind of God - then, and only then, will you be ready to make a choice and do something about that desire so that it bears fruit.

At that point you won't be satisfied with the meagre offerings of teaching once a week on Sundays. When you get that kind of hunger for God's Word, I would not be able to satisfy it with ten sermons a week. Friend, if you remember nothing else from this chapter, please remember what I am about to share with you. It's a formula. I usually hate formulas, but this one is guaranteed. This one you can take to the bank. This formula will affect every area of your life:

$$\frac{\textbf{Desire + Choice + Commitment}}{\textbf{Prayer}} = \text{SUCCESS}$$

If you really want something and choose to pursue it moment by moment, day by day; and are willing to pay the price with your commitment; and that whole process is saturated and guided by God in prayer … then you will succeed! You will see the desires of your heart fulfilled – that is a 100% guarantee.

Now I can hear the question already. *"What if our desires are not God's desires? Surely, we can't expect to succeed unless we know God's will first."* Excellent question again! That is where prayer comes in. The whole process is birthed and covered in prayer. As you humbly and consistently seek the face of God, any ungodly desires; any desires that are not in line with His plan for you right at that time, will be replaced with new desires by His Holy Spirit.

It really is that simple. I pray this way all the time. *"Lord, give me the desires of my heart - or change those desires so they align with Yours."*

I hear other questions: *"What if you know you should desire something, but it just doesn't come? What if you know that you should want to be a committed disciple - and want to see your city transformed and really want to make a difference - but you can't seem to connect to that desire in your heart at present?"*

Now that's a tricky one but it also strikes at the very heart of the matter and reveals a dilemma in the modern Church. What if the desire for the deeper things of God is just not there? What if all this revival stuff sounds great but it just doesn't ring your bell?

Well, I'm afraid I can only offer two possible explanations for that. I can see only two reasons why someone who professes to be a believer would be devoid of the desire to be a real disciple.

(a) You are not born-again and only think you are a Christian. Therefore, we need to pray over you and let God's saving power touch and transform your heart.

(b) You are born-again but you have made choices which have repelled the manifest presence of God in your life, and you have backslidden into a form of godliness that lacks power.

Either way, such a person needs prayer! The first one needs the Holy Spirit to lead them to the point of embracing the salvation Jesus died to give them. The second one needs God's spirit to convict them of their backsliding and empower their fresh choice and commitment to really follow Jesus.

Jesus said in John 10:10 that He came that we might have life to the full ... 'abundant' life some translations call it. So, let me ask you, is your life *abundant* today? Is your life overflowing with fruit and purpose and passion and blessing? The answer should be YES because that's what God desires! That's why Jesus came.

If your life is not full to overflowing it is probably because you don't want that more than anything else ... or you want it, but you have not made the choice to pursue it .... or you have not made the commitment to persevere, pay the price and see it through. Jesus told us how wild and crazy our desires should be. He told us to pray something outrageous. He said to pray, "*your kingdom come, your will be done on earth as it is in heaven.*"

Do you know what that means? It means that you and I are to pray for and believe God for the reality of the kingdom of heaven to increasingly become a reality in us, through us and in the world around us. So, all the needs we see and the shortcomings we experience in this broken, fallen, world will gradually be overpowered by the reality of God's Kingdom - where Jesus Christ rules and reigns as King and God's will is always done. That is God's heart's desire, revealed to us in 2 Chronicles 7:14.

God never wanted a dictatorship – He always wanted a partnership.

He always planned to save, redeem and bless His creation with us by His side all the way. There is nothing we need to know that has not already been explained in the Scriptures and taught by millions of faithful preachers down through the ages. God has made it abundantly clear how important this partnership is to Him. We just have to decide how important it is to us.

"*If my people . . . then I will . . .*" has been God's constant refrain throughout all of human history.

Believe it, or not.

CHAPTER TWO

The Key to Everything

We began this important study by looking at a vitally important statement of the Apostle Paul's in his first letter to the Church at Corinth. Let's look at that again for a moment.

> *"By the grace of God I am what I am, and his grace to me was not without effect. No, I worked harder than all of them - yet not I, but the grace of God that was with me." (1 Corinthians 15:10)*

I suggested that just like a double-sided coin, this verse contains two foundational truths which must be held in balance. The first truth states that we are who we are by the grace of God. Understanding God's grace is a vital first step understanding everything else in the Christian life. We must know deep down in our spirit that we did not earn our salvation, we did not deserve it, there is nothing we can do to pay Him back for it.

We were born into a lost and rebellious generation and the condition of sin in which we found ourselves, separated us from the experience of God's love and we were powerless to do anything about it. Then God broke the power of sin, death and Satan through the life, death, and resurrection of Jesus.

There are thousands of people following God today who are still not personally familiar with this side of the coin … and until they are … flipping the coin to the other side will not serve them or their God at all. If you think you would like to know more about God's grace, then I would really encourage you to put this book down and read my first book, *Amazing Grace*.

Now assuming you <u>do</u> have a reasonable grasp on God's grace, let me now flip the coin and tell you that whilst God's grace is unconditional in that we do not need to do anything to earn it, deserve it or receive it, we have to understand that the *effect* of God's grace is conditional upon our choices and effort. Look at Paul's words again.

"By the grace of God, I am what I am …"

Hallelujah … God is good … I don't deserve it … nothing I do or don't do will alter God's love and grace toward me.

"but … his grace to me was not without effect …"

I didn't just receive it, enjoy it and feel warm and mushy inside because of it … it had an effect in my life. Why? Why was this grace effective for Paul?

"… because I worked harder than all of them."

Paul is effectively saying: *"This wonderful free grace of God that has been lavished upon me has been effective … it has borne fruit … it has actually done what it was meant to do … **because I made a choice** to work hard, in partnership with God."*

Then of course, just to maintain the balance Paul reminds us that even our efforts are empowered ultimately by God – as he says,

" … yet not I, but the grace of God that was with me."

In Jesus' name please get this - it is a vital key to the power and glory and reality of life within God's kingdom. This is the key to an effective, abundant Christian life. Let me give you a sentence that will appear to be a riddle at first - but it will make a lot of sense when you understand what I mean by it.

Our efforts are ineffective in securing God's grace, but God's grace is ineffective without our efforts.

This is what Paul is saying. This is also what Paul proved in his life and ministry. Our salvation, our right standing before God, our forgiveness and cleansing, His gifts and power … the whole wonderful package of the gospel is given to us FREE - by His grace - no strings attached - no effort on our part to secure it. In fact, God secured it for us long before we were even born! That's the first side of the coin and you may know that side very well - it is polished and well-worn, and you could articulate the truths contained on that side of the coin to most people.

However, the other side of the coin is equally important and too often neglected by those who think they understand grace. It is the side which says that this grace will be ineffective in the mission of Christ if we do not make deliberate and daily choices which open the channel for God's grace to flow *through* us - rather than just *to* us.

That's why Paul mentions God's grace and his hard work in the same breath: this is a partnership. It is for freedom that Christ has set us free (Gal. 5:1) – freedom is an end itself as far as our relationship with God is concerned. However, we also need to understand that we have been set free for a purpose. God wants us to *respond* to His grace and be *channels* of His grace to a lost and needy world.

This pattern is found all the way through the Bible. We read of God's grace, love, mercy, forbearance, and forgiveness - then almost in the same paragraph we are faced with the question, *"How then shall I live?"* In other words, what is my *response* to what God has done? What choices am I making each day so that what God has put in me – gets out and makes a difference in my life and the lives of those around me?

Let me give you a nice worldly, down-to-earth illustration that we could all relate to. Imagine for a moment (it will be a nice moment, I'm sure), that I deposited ten million dollars into your bank account today. The transaction is legal and there are no strings attached. This is a free gift. It is all yours. You can do with it as you wish. You are the legal owner of every one of those ten million little gifts.

If, and I stress that little word now, *if* you choose to use that money and spend it, then you will not only be the legal owner of the money, but it will *also* have an *effect* in your life. There may be a few people in the world who would leave that money in the bank and never touch it, but I am sure you would agree that the vast majority of normal people would want that money to have an effect in their life. They would want to see the fruit of their gift. They would want to see it make a difference in their world.

Well at some point in eternity, God deposited far more than ten million dollars into your account. He made a whole range of deposits! He deposited unconditional forgiveness; amazing grace; mercy; holiness; righteousness; abundant life; eternal life; a whole bankroll of spiritual gifts; power; glory; majesty; healing; wholeness; peace; love; joy; patience; kindness; goodness; self-control … and the list goes on!

That's quite an impressive bank statement! In fact, the bottom line of your statement actually reads: *The Life of Christ* - and all those things I just mentioned, and more, came in Christ. What you received in this heavenly direct transfer is worth a thousand times more than all money in the world. Money is great, we may all wish we had more, however the deposits God made into our spiritual bank account are worth infinitely more.

But those deposits are only useful and effective if you *choose* to use them. They will only have an effect in your life and through your life for others if you choose to get them out of the bank and into your life choices each and every day.

IF is such a tiny word, but what a power it contains! All through history this tiny word has made such a huge difference in life. All through the Bible we see this word. It shouldn't have all that much power. It's just a two-letter word. But this little word punches above its weight because once it begins a sentence, it controls everything that follows. Its power is disproportionate to its size.

Sometimes I think when we read the Bible, we just ignore this little word. We seem really good at embracing the 'then' parts. We preach about them and cry out to God for the 'then' promises … but we disconnect them from the 'if' parts. We read right through the book of Genesis; through the prophets; the Psalms, the minor prophets; into the gospels; then the epistles. On every page, we so easily ignore this tiny word. The problem is that 'if' just won't go away. It's right there in our face all through the Old and New Testaments.

One of the most powerful sentences in the whole Bible, and the verse which provides the framework for this book, begins with this little word.

"If my people, who are called by my name, will humble themselves and pray and seek my face and turn from their wicked ways, then will I hear from heaven and will forgive their sin and will heal their land." (2 Chronicles 7:14)

God will do what He has promised - if His people respond to His love and grace and blessing. This big little word is all through the Bible. It's in the Garden of Eden. It's in the story of Cain and Abel. It's in the story of Moses and Abraham and every other great man and woman of God. This big little word is all through history. We live in a cause-and-effect world which is dominated by this *'if ... then'* reality.

I am definitely not talking about a performance-based rewards system here. I am not talking about God just rewarding us for our efforts. I am talking about a more practical and pragmatic reality. I am simply pointing out that God has set us totally and completely free to choose life or death; heaven or hell, right or wrong, this colour car or that colour car; this Church or that Church. We are free to choose.

Yes, God is sovereign - I affirm that. I actually have a very high view of God's sovereignty - but as a sovereign God He can do whatever He wants, and what He wants for you and me and all His children is absolutely amazing and just a little terrifying at times. Our sovereign God chose to channel His sovereignty into the choices of His beloved children. He so desperately wanted a free relationship of love with us, He set us completely free.

We are free to sin, or not sin.

We are free to obey, or not obey.

We are free to worship, or not worship.

We are free to use the spiritual gifts He gives, or ignore them.

We are free to reach out into our communities and change lives every day, or stay safe within our fortress and die on the vine.

We are free to believe what God says so clearly, or ignore it and make up theologies which suit our personal agendas.

We are free to receive the riches of heaven in salvation, and then do absolutely nothing with them.

God really wants us to love Him, serve Him and fulfil His great commission and the mission of Christ because we <u>want</u> to … not because we <u>have</u> to. That is why He set us totally free. That is why there are hundreds of *"If … then"* pleas from God all the way through the Bible. Each one of those statements affirms our freedom to choose and affirms what God can and will do IF we choose to let Him.

It is quite bizarre how we read the Bible and see all the wonderful 'then' promises, but miss the big 'if' which usually precedes most of them, and then we wonder why God doesn't appear to answer us when we cry out for healing and revival and intimacy.

The fabric of our faith must be woven together not only with God's grace, but also with the resulting obedience and action on our part which allows that grace to have an effect. We don't want it to be that way. We want God's promises to be effective without us. We want to just sit back, and watch God do His stuff – with us in the grandstand cheering *"Go God … Go God …!!"*

We want to read scripture from Genesis to Revelation, ignoring the big 'if.' But this big little word is there, on almost every page and in every paragraph. *"If my people will … then I will …"*

Do we understand the power of this word? It can't be outvoted by popular opinion. It can't be outflanked by policy. Nothing can change this 'if' because it's God's 'if.' If we do what we're asked to do and what we were created to do, then all the promises of God will unfold and bear fruit before our very eyes. We will cash cheques on our heavenly bank account every day and we will really make a difference IF … and only IF … we do it God's way.

Let me share a couple of stories from real life:

A man and his family were going camping. They came across a sign that said, "*Road Closed. Do Not Enter.*" The man just drove around the sign because had checked the map and he was sure it would save them time on their journey. Some men are like that … especially when on vacation … they need to get from point A to point B by a certain time and that means no stopping to smell the roses and no turning back because of some warning sign. So, this guy just drove right around the sign.

His wife was very resistant to going around that sign. She was cautious. She was wise. But there was no stopping this persistent road warrior. After a few kilometres of successful navigation, now quite happy with his decision to ignore the road sign, he began to boast of his gift of discernment. He knew there wasn't anything wrong with the road. Someone just put that sign there. Whatever it was, it was nothing big enough to stop him.

It wasn't long before he broke out in a humble sweat as he looked up ahead at a washed-out bridge. He turned the car around and retraced his tracks back to the main road. He didn't save time. He lost heaps of time.

When they arrived at the original warning sign he was greeted by a large hand-painted message on the back side of the sign. His wife and three children all read the hand-painted sign out loud. It said: "*Welcome back, stupid!*"

That's the way it is with God's master plan for His children. God's word answers the age-old question, "*How then shall we live?*" He lays out the boundaries and erects all the road signs and IF we observe them … IF we actually listen to God and let <u>Him</u> guide our path … THEN our lives will work, and we will make a huge difference in this life and the next.

IF we cross over those boundaries or ignore the signs however, THEN we reap the consequences. Terrible things happen when we go places we really shouldn't go.

There was one lady on vacation who went up a mountain she should have avoided. No one would have blamed her had she stayed behind. At twelve below zero, even Frosty the Snowman would have opted for a warm fire. Hardly a day for snow skiing, but her husband was - like our other friend - very insistent, and so she went.

While waiting on the lift, she realized she needed a restroom! Her husband assured her there would be a restroom at the top of the lift. She endured the ride with great torture - a bouncy ride - only to discover at the top there was no such facility. She panicked.

Her husband had an idea: Why not go into the woods? Since she was wearing an all-white outfit, she'd blend in with the snow. And what better powder room than a piney grove? What choice did she have? She skied past the tree line and arranged her ski suit at half-mast. I'm sure you get the picture. Fortunately, no one could see her.

Unfortunately, her husband hadn't told her to remove her skis. Before you could blink, she was streaking backwards down the slope, revealing more about herself than she ever intended. (After all, hindsight is 20/20.) With arms flailing and skis sailing, she sped under the very lift she'd just ridden and collided with a large pylon.

She scrambled to cover the essentials and discovered her arm was broken. Fortunately, her husband raced to her rescue. He summoned the ski patrol, who transported her to the hospital. While being treated in the emergency room, a man with a broken leg was carried in and placed next to her. By now she'd regained her composure enough to make small talk. "*So, how'd you break your leg?*" she asked.

"*It was the darndest thing you ever saw,*" he explained. "*I was riding up the ski lift and suddenly I couldn't believe my eyes. There was this crazy half naked woman skiing backwards, at top speed. I leaned over to get a better look and I fell out of the lift.*" Then he turned to her and asked, "*So how did you break your arm?*"

We make the same mistake, don't we? We climb mountains we are never intended to climb. We choose to go up when we should have stayed down. As a result, we take nasty spills in view of the whole world as it watches us fall in our folly. We, too, end up bruised, embarrassed, and exposed when we don't follow the clear path that God has laid out before us.

Now you might be thinking to yourself at this point ... *"He's reading from the Old Testament. What about the New Testament? In the Old Testament, God is a God of law. But in the New Testament, God is a God of grace. Unconditional grace. The big `if' is absent from the New Testament."* Not so. The big IF is all the way through the New Testament. Yes, the grace and mercy of God is far more pronounced in the New Testament and yes, the grace of God which saves us is unconditional in the sense that it is in no way a reward for our performance or the quality of our obedience. That is all true and I have taught those truths for over forty years and will continue to teach them until my last breath!

However, the *effect* of God's grace and mercy and forgiveness *is* conditional. Firstly, we have to *believe* it ... that is our choice and secondly, we have to *act on what we believe* and allow it to manifest in observable ways in our lives.

We can rejoice in the fact that we are saved and redeemed and reconciled to God and that by His grace we are bound for heaven. But we still live in a cause-and-effect reality. The choices we make will have a direct bearing on what God can do in our life, in our city and in this whole nation.

Remember the statement I made earlier? *Our efforts are ineffective in securing God's grace, but God's grace is ineffective without our efforts.* IF we cash a cheque against our ten-million-dollar bank account, it will change the way we live and we will get to see the fruit of those riches. IF we cash a cheque against the bank of heaven ... that is, if we make daily choices which are consistent with the revealed will of God and His plan for His children, then it will change the way we live, and we will see the incredible, eternal fruit of those choices.

The big IF. No matter how much we'd like to get rid of it, it looms large in the text. We must begin with that big little word, it is a gateway to all the glory and riches and nation-transforming power of heaven ... or it is a roadblock in our whole journey with God. Everything we hope for and everything we ever dreamed of, hinges on what we do with that one big little word: IF

IF you decide to let that word be a gateway to the abundant life God has planned for you; IF you decide you want to know what choices you need to make on the other side of that gate, THEN read on in this book as we continue our examination of the verse which is the catalyst for all that I have written here.

> *"**If** my people, who are called by my name, will humble themselves and pray and seek my face and turn from their wicked ways, **then** will I hear from heaven and will forgive their sin and will heal their land." (2 Chronicles 7:14)*

This is a truly powerful and confronting verse which sums up every IF in the whole Bible. It is a verse which contains many truths about God and us, which, when unpacked and applied, can and will change our whole lives. But that will not happen ... that will not begin to happen until we get past that first word IF.

Are you prepared to pay the price and go through that gateway?

Are you prepared to fulfil your end of this amazing partnership with God?

Are you prepared to make the choices necessary to unleash the riches and power and glory of heaven in your life, in your church and in your nation?

Spend some time with the Lord soon and let Him reveal your heart. Only then will you be able to discover the answers to those really important questions.

CHAPTER THREE

A Small but Powerful Word

In the last chapter I spent a lot of time talking about the first word of this challenging verse:

> *"If my people, who are called by my name, will humble themselves and pray and seek my face and turn from their wicked ways, then will I hear from heaven and will forgive their sin and will heal their land." (2 Chronicles 7:14)*

It may seem strange to spend a whole chapter on one tiny word, it hardly seems worthy of such attention, does it? However, as I have already stated – this one little word, IF, when placed at the beginning of a sentence, has complete control over everything that follows. It is a word which carries tremendous power and should attract far more of our attention than it does. So I really think this small but powerful word needs two chapters!

The reason we don't spend too much time meditating on this big little word is that we are too busy focusing on the word that usually follows later in the sentence: THEN. IF you do a certain thing, THEN a certain consequence will follow. This is just the natural cause-and-effect reality which we see in every area of life.

⇒ IF you put your hand in the fire, THEN you will be burned.

⇒ IF you walk out onto a crowded highway with your eyes closed, THEN you will get run over.

⇒ IF you get more sleep, THEN you will be better able to meet the challenges of the day.

⇒ IF you save some money, THEN you will be able to pay for those unexpected expenses which occur from time to time.

⇒ IF you drive too fast, THEN one day, eventually, you will have an accident, and someone will be injured or killed.

Every day in so many ways, you and I encounter these 'if-then' realities. These are examples of the thousands of fundamental cause-and-effect realities which govern life. They are so simple and so obvious that you are probably wondering why I would even bother pointing them out. Well, I want us to start simple and remember that this process *is* simple and it's also irrefutable. I want you nodding early in the chapter as you agree with these really basic cause-and-effect realities of life because the further we go, the harder it will become for you to keep nodding!

Your actions have consequences. This is true whether you are a Christian, a Buddhist, a Muslim or an atheist. There is nothing particularly spiritual about what I am telling you at this point. This is just the way all life on earth is. We make choices and there are consequences which follow. Things we do and things we choose to not do will always have consequences.

Of course, Christians certainly have an enormous advantage in that some of our choices are empowered by God and therefore they can be far more significant and fruitful … but they are still our choices.

God cannot and will not make our choices for us.

Many of these cause-and-effect choices are quite superficial and relatively insignificant to life, but many others affect us at the core of our being and that's why I started simple at first - because the other choices are more far more confronting.

For example: IF you choose to ignore the clear truth of the Gospel and reject the free gift of salvation offered freely by God, THEN you will spend eternity separated from the reality of God's love and grace and presence.

IF you choose to believe that God loves you and has opened a way through Jesus Christ whereby you can be re-united with your Creator in a wonderful, life-changing, eternal encounter, THEN you'll experience all the power, majesty, victory and beauty of life as God intended it to be.

Choices and consequences - they surround us everywhere, don't they? This is as true in the church as it is outside the church. In fact, I would suggest that this 'IF - THEN' reality is even more applicable for Christians because we have already been totally and wonderfully set free in Christ and God has returned the freedom of choice given to mankind when we were created.

Look up the words *free* and *freedom* in a New Testament concordance and read how many verses there are which remind us of our freedom of choice and the various consequences to each one of those choices. Some are liberating and life-changing, others are devastating and destructive.

Now you may ask, *"Isn't God sovereign? As Christians, are we not aware that there is a higher power Who controls everything? Surely Christians worship a God who is able to do anything He wants ... regardless of our choices. Unlike the world, we are in submission to a higher power and if our sovereign God wants to do something ... He will just do it ... regardless of our choices."*

Do you realise that there are millions of sincere, Godly men and women all over the world who would say a hearty AMEN to what I just wrote? I guarantee some of you are reading this book. These are genuine disciples of Jesus who sincerely believe that if God wants to do something He will just do it - regardless of our choices. Why these people believe this I will never know.

Why Christians all over world choose to park their brains when they come to Jesus defies me, it really does. Our thoughts run our lives; what we think will in a large measure determine how we live. IF our thoughts are wrong, THEN our lives will be wrong! So many people in the church have lost the ability, or given up the responsibility, to reason and judge and analyse and weigh up truth and logic and common sense.

When they encounter teaching or practices which they may not agree with or understand or accept, they switch to this 'spiritual mode' and float off with the fairies somewhere saying, *"God will reveal His truth to me, I just need to pray."*

By all means, pray about everything, God exhorts us to do just that - but the same God said, *"Come, let us reason together."* The same God tells us that we will be transformed by the renewing of our mind. He doesn't tell us to sell our brains for spare parts when we come into His Kingdom! The vast majority of problems we have in understanding God and His will and our purpose in that will would disappear if we would just THINK more clearly about our faith and work through things logically and sensibly.

Of course, we should pray ... but that should not be our first response. Please listen carefully here - I do not want to lose you here because you think I have a low view of prayer - I have a very high view of prayer and you will see that later in this book. Prayer is wonderful. Prayer is essential. However, prayer should never be a place we run to and hide when we don't want to use our brain! There are many, many times when God does not want us to run to Him straight away – He wants us to THINK first and recall what He has already told us!

When we were little children, we asked our parents a hundred questions a day and many of them were ridiculously basic and simple. As we matured, our parents encouraged us to think for ourselves and work out the answers to many of those questions based on our own experience, using our own minds to reason, assess, evaluate, and examine all aspects of a situation. That's called growing up. That's a mark of maturity.

Christians need to mature in exactly the same way in their spiritual lives. There will be things we simply have to ask God because our experience and the clear teaching He has already given us in the Bible may not be enough for us to work it out ourselves. However (in Jesus' name please get this!), the vast majority of stuff I hear coming out of the mouths of Christians (including my own some days), in our prayers and petitions to God is a total waste of time and a clear indication that we have lost the ability to think! We still run to Daddy with some of the most basic, childish, ignorant requests – all of which have already been answered by Him over and over and over again in the Bible, in a thousand sermons and in our own life's experience!

If we would just stop, think, and work it out with some anointed common sense, we would not get ourselves into so many of the complicated situations and debates we do, and we would be a hundred times more effective as disciples of Christ. We cry out to God for intimacy. *"I want to know you more, Lord, I want to hear your voice and know your presence and power and glory."* If I had a dollar for every time I have heard that kind of prayer, I would be a very rich man. Yet God has clearly told us that this highly coveted, rarely experienced intimacy is actually ours for the taking. We don't need to beg Him for it - it is freely available to every child of God. Intimacy with God is not just a *prayer* away, intimacy with God is just a *choice* away!

James tells us more clearly than anyone when he says, *"Draw near to God and He will draw near to you."* (James 4:8). There's another IF – THEN statement and a very powerful one at that. It just doesn't use those words. But it effectively does: IF you make a deliberate, daily choice to live and act in a way which attracts God's real presence, THEN God will visit you in the most intimate, personal, powerful way - every day of your life.

I cannot find a clearer statement in the whole Bible which, if understood, will instantly remove a backlog of millions of useless prayers which appear to be unanswered by God. Well, it appears to us that they are unanswered prayers because we still do not have the intimacy we pray for. God most definitely answered those prayers - He answered them long before we prayed them by showing us very clearly in the Bible how we might achieve that place of deep communion with Himself.

Our experience also tells us the answer and renders our prayers unnecessary. Genuine disciples know from their own journey as they reflect on those special times when God seemed really near to them. I guarantee that if they analyse their own actions and choices before and during those times of intimacy, they will realise that they chose to do and not do certain things which allowed them to 'draw near to God' and He was faithful to them and He drew near to them in a powerful way. Cause and effect; if - then; it really is that simple.

We cry out to God for renewal in the church and revival in our land. *"Please God, we beg You to come and heal our land and reconcile Your lost people to Yourself. We cry out to You for our city, Lord, for the salvation of every man, woman, and child; we beseech Thee Father to send us revival by Your sovereign hand!"* If I had just 5 cents for every revival prayer being praying across this nation just today, I would be an instant millionaire.

So, what's wrong with praying for revival? Nothing is wrong with praying for revival … IF … you know how God plans to answer that prayer and as long as you know the implications of that prayer. Unless you know what brings revival, don't pray for it, because you will not like how God answers your prayer. Just like you may not be liking what I am saying right now in this book because I am focusing on you and your choices and that usually makes people squirm a little.

Well, it may come as a shock to some people, but teaching like this *is* the answer to your prayers for revival. There has been a growing ache in people's hearts for revival in recent days and I have heard many people around me praying for God to move in power and bring that revival.

Well, if you are one of those people, be encouraged - God is listening. God has heard your prayers and now He is answering them. Revival is coming and I am here to tell you exactly how. If you have been crying out for revival, then God is answering you right now. Listen to His voice now. This is what He is saying:

> *"I am bringing that revival … it is already on its way … and IF My people, who are petitioning Me day and night for revival … will humble themselves and deal with that ugly pride in their hearts … and commit time to seeking My face instead of My favours … if they deal ruthlessly with the sin which still lurks in their hearts which, although forgiven and atoned for in My eyes, continues to attract the ministry of doubt, discouragement, deception, darkness and death … if My people would just do those few simple things over a sustained period of time, THEN transformation (not just revival) will most certainly come."*

We cry out to God to release the reality of so many 'THEN' promises in our lives and across our nation, but we continue to ignore all the 'IF' components to the fulfilment of those promises. Which brings me right back to that statement I made earlier which I believe many Christians would support and that is: If our sovereign God wants to do something ... He will just do it ... regardless of our choices.

Let's switch our brain on and actually think about that for one minute ... that's all it will take. This is not a deep theological issue - this is just a simple logical issue. This is not a debate about the sovereignty of God - this is simply a clear examination of truth and the experience of mankind throughout history.

God will do what God wants to do? OK let's start there. What does God want to do? We know this already ... this is not a trick question. The Bible so clearly reveals God's heart on a thousand issues - let's pick a few shall we? Does God want everyone to embrace the gift of salvation secured for them in Christ? You'd better believe it! The Bible says it is not God's will that any remain outside the knowledge and experience of His love and grace. Well, are there people in the world today who still haven't embraced their salvation in Christ? Yes. How long has it been God's will to save them? Thousands of years! So here is one thing that God wants - that isn't happening.

Does God want you to know His will, hear His voice and walk in harmony with Him every moment of every day? Yes, of course He does ... He has said so many times. Well, is that your current experience? Is that how you are living now? Do you hear God's voice clearly, above your own and others and Satan's ... all the time ... every day? No? Well, there is something else that God wants - and is not getting at present.

Does God want the power and reality of the Kingdom of Heaven to flood our current world and sweep all of us into the river of abundant, eternal life? Of course, He does! Jesus Himself told us to pray that the Kingdom of God would come and flood our current reality so that what is true in heaven becomes true in our experience right here and now.

Well, are there still sick people in our city? Are there lost and lonely people in our city? Are there sad, defeated, broken and bruised people in our city? Yes, of course, there are! Well, God is not getting what He wants, is He? So, to say that our Sovereign God will simply do whatever He wants regardless of our choices is simply not true, is it? Why is that the case? Why is God not getting what He wants?

You know why … deep down in our hearts we all know why. We just don't want to think about it. We just don't want to accept that **our choices can determine whether God gets what He wants or not.** God wants our lives to work and be victorious, effective, fruitful and fun! But we continue to make choices which cut across His desire and His will. This 'IF – THEN' dynamic will just not go away! So let's stop fighting it!

IF you choose to accept what God is teaching you now and start to evaluate every one of your choices and your responses and your behaviours *before* you cry out to God for a miracle cure that does not involve you making better choices, THEN you will have travelled a long way in your journey to see your life and your community transformed.

These annoying 'IF – THEN' realities are everywhere! You can ignore them if you like, but they will still be there. IF you believe that God chose to channel His life-changing power through the choices of His people, THEN hopefully you will start to make better choices so that will happen in and through you!

IF you believe that God is truly able to do immeasurably more than all we ask or imagine, THEN you will rise above the worst circumstances and the greatest attacks of the enemy and you will know Christ's victory on a daily basis. IF you choose to let the pressures of life and the actions of others hurt you or offend you or upset you for more than a minute or de-rail you from your journey into the heart and purposes of God, THEN you will, by your own choice, become a victim who sucks the life out of people as you expect them to hold your hand and comfort you whilst you wallow in self-pity and pride.

IF you choose to believe the clear teaching of Scripture and the testimony of thousands of people who live out those Scriptures; that God has called us into partnership with Himself and that the transformation of our nation is as much in our hands as it is in His, THEN you will understand that nothing will change in this until you and I and all the people who bear the name of Jesus make some different choices each day.

God is not going to fix this without us! Why do you think we are still here more than 2,000 years after Jesus came to wind all this up and save the world? Is God slow? Has He lost His touch? Was saving the world a little ambitious for even God? Or does that delay in seeing the Kingdom of God advance and drive out the kingdom of darkness have something to do with us and our responses and our choices and our wrong thinking and our stubborn refusal to do what He has clearly called us to do?

IF you choose to give God and His people and His ministry and teaching only a fraction of your time, energy and devotion each week, THEN you will stagnate spiritually, lose the ability to hear from God and become an obstacle to step around in the church rather than a vital part of His Kingdom ministry.

IF your choices are always governed by your personal needs and desires, THEN God will not be able to use you in any significant way in His Kingdom and you will not make a difference in this life at all and will probably be a pain to everyone around you.

IF you choose to believe this day that you have the ability to open a door to the radical, spiritual and socio-political transformation of this whole nation, and IF you have a passion for God's will to be done here as it is in heaven, THEN you will see the desires of your heart fulfilled in your community and you will join the thousands of other communities across the world where God's transforming power is being released right now … through the choices of His people … as God does for us what He promised to do for his people thousands of years ago: He will heal our land.

CHAPTER FOUR
To Whom is God Speaking?

I want to really encourage you to go back and spend some time going through the first three chapters in this book. The last two were spent looking at the serious implications of the very first word of 2 Chronicles 7:14. That word is 'if.' I never would have thought that one tiny word like that could have such an impact – but it does.

The first word of this verse is a key to the whole thrust of what God is saying here. Now we shall look at the next few words. They tell us to whom this verse is addressed and therefore, given its context, they tell us who God intends to use to heal the land.

*"If **My people**, who are **called by My name** ..."*

God is talking to His own chosen people here. In our context, living this side of the cross of Christ, God would be talking to Christians – the people who bear the name of Christ and the people who are called by God to fulfil the mission of Christ.

Collectively, therefore, God is talking to the church – which means that individually, He is talking to you and me and anyone else who claims to belong to Him. So what? Is this important? Absolutely! The fact that God is talking to us – the church of Jesus Christ – is both amazing and terrifying all at once! It's amazing because it shows us, yet again, how incredible God's plan is. We should be honoured, humbled and empowered by the revelation that the church of Jesus Christ holds the key to all the problems in the world. In fact, the Apostle Paul tells us in Ephesians 3:10 that God's intent in these last days is that through the Church, the manifold wisdom of God will be made known to the rulers and authorities in the heavenly realms.

How amazing is that? God is going to use you and me to instruct angels and demons in the heavenly realms!

It's also terrifying to realise that God's people who are called by His name carry the responsibility for the state of our nation! The condition of our 'land' is directly linked to the health, obedience and effectiveness of the church.

This verse, and many like it throughout the Bible, leave us with little doubt that if our nation; if our city is struggling in any way then the *first* place to look for the solution is the church of Jesus Christ – the people of God.

Some would even go so far as to say that the church is the place to look for the *cause* of society's problems in the sense that our refusal to really be the people God called us to be is the reason why evil has taken over the world. I am not sure if I would go that far … but it's a sobering thought!

At the very least, we have to face the truth that Jesus came over 2,000 years ago to usher in the Kingdom of Heaven, the rule and reign of the King, and He commanded and empowered His disciples to do the same through the Great Commission. God gave us *everything we need* for life and Godliness (2 Peter 1:3); everything we need to bring God's lost children home; and here we are thousands of years later still trying to work out what God's will is as we so cleverly and boldly shirk our responsibility for the condition of our city and our nation.

If the church had really taken hold of the confronting principles wrapped up in 2 Chronicles 7:14 and hundreds of other clear exhortations in both Old and New Testaments which so clearly define our role as God's people in saving the world; if the church had embraced the very clear mandate we have been given by God to drive out the enemy from this land and take back what he has stolen - then, your life and mine and the world around us would be very different today.

If the people of God had taken the Word of God seriously then we would have grown up and moved on to the meat, taken this city and nation for Jesus and gone home to glory many years ago!

When I examine the clear teaching of the New Testament and discover the strength of the mandate Jesus gave us to go and make disciples; when I am reminded on almost every page that we are indwelt by the same life and power which created this whole universe; when I look at the technology, resources and opportunities which God has poured out upon His people – particularly over the last 100 years - I have to accept the fact that we, the church, have dropped the ball in so many ways.

I firmly believe that we could have (and should have) all been in heaven by now. For many, many years the people of God have had the mission and the means to see the whole world brought to its knees before Jesus Christ. The only reason that has not happened is because we have not had God's motive – we have not really wanted what God wants. The ache in our heart for the salvation of everyone in our city and our nation has simply not been strong enough.

Whether we like it or not, at some point we need to take a long hard look in the mirror and accept that we may be more interested in our personal needs, the needs of our family and our Church family, than we are in fulfilling the purposes in God. Jesus came to seek and to save the lost; He came to usher in the kingdom of Heaven - the rule and reign of God; He came to shine the light of God into every dark corner of our society; He came to be the salt of the earth - to preserve the precious children of God. This same Jesus said, *"As I have been sent – so I am sending you."* This same Jesus also said, *"… and even greater things than these shall you do in my name."*

So why is it not happening? Well, actually it is happening – in a growing number of places all around the world – God is being faithful to His Word, and he is healing whole cities and entire nations. But why is it not happening yet in nations like Australia who are still awaiting such a move of God? We know the answer. This is not really a difficult question - we are just not comfortable with the answer because it has very personal implications. The answer is in 2 Chronicles 7:14 and it has been staring at us our whole lives!

Do you realise that God had already given us the answer to every problem our nation would ever face – centuries before we faced them? How simple is that? It's all there - laid out for us in Bible. There are hundreds of instructions and exhortations and keys to success for any and every nation. Everywhere you turn there is another insight which impinges upon the health and prosperity of this nation.

Yet it is even simpler than that … the whole lot could be summed up by saying **if you have a healthy church, you will have a healthy nation.** If the church is operating as it was meant to operate, then every nation in the world will operate as they were meant to operate.

It all comes back to the people of God – the 'chosen ones' – the 'elect' – the 'sons and daughters of God' – the 'household of faith' – the 'army of God' – the 'family of God' … those people whom we call Christians – or better still 'Disciples of Jesus Christ.' The ball appears to be in our court. The spotlight of Scripture and history is deliberately aimed at the people whom God calls His own. They are the source of His affection and the means by which He will accomplish His purpose.

So, if we are concerned about the state of our nation, according to the Bible, we should not look to the politicians and national leaders - the first place we should look is the church. God has not promised to heal the land through the choices of politicians and social leaders. God said He would heal the land through the choices made by His people who are called by His name.

Therefore, before we even begin to look at those choices … before we even start to explore what it might mean for the people of God to humble themselves, pray, seek His face, and repent - we first need to establish who are the people of God.

More specifically, you need to ask yourself today: *"Am I one of them? Am I really part of the people of God? When God says, 'If my People …' do I know without any doubt that He is talking about me?"*

If your answer is a resounding *"Yes!"* then I ask you, on what basis do you make that assessment? How does one know if they are part of God's people? Well, many would say you just know. The Spirit of God witnesses to your spirit, and you just know, because you know, because you know! I happen to believe there is a lot of merit in that statement, but is that all that God has provided as proof that we really belong to Him? Or is there some more objective criteria for assessing our true spiritual position? Thankfully, there is.

In Acts 16:31 we read where Paul and Silas are in jail and the jailer asks the magic question: *"What must I do to be saved?"* and Paul replied with a powerful, yet simple statement: *"Believe in the Lord Jesus Christ and you shall be saved."* So, is that the criteria for being the people of God? Simply believe in the Lord Jesus Christ? Yes, that is, in essence, the door that leads you to the reality of the Kingdom of God.

However, we must understand something here which can slip past us in the simplicity of this verse. The phrase 'believe in' is obviously the key here but unfortunately our modern understanding of this concept is quite different to its original meaning in this verse.

In our day and age, to believe in something does not necessarily impact us personally or profoundly. We can acknowledge the reality of something; even the importance of something; give intellectual assent to something – without that belief having any real impact in our lives. Not so in this verse and not so anywhere in the New Testament where this kind of language is used.

The Greek word used here, which we translate 'believe in,' happens to be far stronger in its meaning. It literally should be translated 'believe into' and it carries the connotation of diving into a deep pool of water and being totally immersed and saturated in the process.

That is another reason why Baptism is such a powerful symbol, because it depicts our total commitment to the Lord Jesus Christ; our absolute surrender to Him.

When the Bible says, 'believe in the Lord Jesus Christ' it is not saying 'subscribe to His teaching and theological perspective.' It is not saying, 'give intellectual, arms-length assent to His claims to be the Son of God and the saviour of the world.' It must start there. It has to start there. What we think will affect how we live, so our thoughts about God and ourselves are very important and any belief in Jesus must have that component to it.

However, when the Bible says 'believe in Jesus' it means far more than a mental agreement to a principle. It means dive in, fully, completely and without hesitation. Immerse yourself totally in the person and purpose of this Jesus. Just as the water would surround you, soak you and saturate you ... so too with Jesus when you 'believe INTO Him.'

So, when Paul uttered those famous words, *"Believe in the Lord Jesus Christ and you shall be saved,"* he had no concept of this being an intellectual belief; this was a 'boots and all, no holds barred, all or nothing, dive into the river and get wet' belief! He knew of no other. So how can you tell if someone has that kind of belief and is a disciple of Jesus and part of His church? Well, let's look at some more Scripture. Let's see if we can find some objective criteria to affirm our position as part of the People of God.

> *"A new command I give you: Love one another. As I have loved you, so you must love one another. By this all men will know that you are my disciples, if you love one another."* (John 13:34-35)

This is self-explanatory. The only question which begs is 'How did Jesus love us?' Well, He laid down his life for us. He gave everything He had in order to see us saved and reconciled to God. So, if we are prepared to lay everything on the line to see God's lost children brought home; if our love is an *action*, like it was with Jesus, and not just some mushy feeling, then I guess we will know that we are part of the 'People of God.'

John builds on this picture beautifully in his first letter. When you have some time, I would really encourage you to read 1 John 4:7–5:13 and see the wonderful assurance we can have that we belong to God and have eternal life.

There is no guesswork here. Our choices and the way we live will reveal if we are really God's children or not. Galatians 5:13-25 is another great passage to read concerning the 'fruit' which is evident in the life of God's chosen children.

Jesus also talked about judging a tree by its fruit. In the same way, we are to assess by the fruit of our lives whether we belong to God and are indwelt by His spirit or not.

> *"Therefore, if anyone is in Christ, he is a new creation; the old has gone, the new has come!" (2 Corinthians 5:17)*

> *"In reply Jesus declared, "I tell you the truth, no one can see the kingdom of God unless he is born again." "How can a man be born when he is old?" Nicodemus asked. "Surely he cannot enter a second time into his mother's womb to be born!" Jesus answered, "I tell you the truth, no one can enter the kingdom of God unless he is born of water and the Spirit. Flesh gives birth to flesh, but the Spirit gives birth to spirit." (John 3:3-6)*

> *"For you have been born again, not of perishable seed, but of imperishable, through the living and enduring word of God." (1 Peter 1:23)*

> *"But you are a chosen people, a royal priesthood, a holy nation, a people belonging to God, that you may declare the praises of him who called you out of darkness into his wonderful light. Once you were not a people, but now you are the people of God; once you had not received mercy, but now you have received mercy. Dear friends, I urge you, as aliens and strangers in the world, to abstain from sinful desires, which war against your soul. Live such good lives among the pagans that, though they accuse you of doing wrong, they may see your good deeds and glorify God on the day he visits us." (1 Peter 2:9-12)*

I could go on for pages because there are hundreds of passages in the Bible which give us objective criteria to judge whether we are the people of God. The bottom line is indisputable: when God comes to town – stuff happens!

When the Spirit of God enters a human life transformation is the result. Things change and this change is not only secretive and personal, but also visible and discernible by those around us. In fact, I would suggest that the most reliable means of determining whether you are a Christian or not; the most guaranteed way of assessing whether you belong to God is to ask someone around you, in your family, in your workplace, anywhere you interact with people one-on-one. Do they see the life of Christ in you? Do those who knew you before you made a profession of faith in Christ notice any difference in you now?

Is the observable fruit in your life the fruit of the flesh or the fruit of the Spirit? Is the overwhelming, unconditional love, grace and mercy of God Himself flowing from you and touching everyone around you? Or do you 'put it on' for church and then revert to the real you when not surrounded by Christians?

We need to be asking these questions. We need to be spending time in front of the mirror of God's Word and not leaving until we really know the person looking back at us and until we face the hard truth about our true spiritual standing. I know of many committed, active, dedicated people working in the church who deep down, are not even sure if they are going to heaven!

We need to know if we belong to God. We need to know if we are the 'my people' God is addressing in 2 Chronicles 7:14 and many other verses in the Bible. We need to face the fact that it is entirely possible to be active in church life for many years and still have an unregenerate heart. We can spend our life serving God and doing wonderful things for Him and still not be born again and indwelt by His Spirit.

The church can easily be a social club where we hang out with our friends, learn the language; give the required responses and answers and fool most of the people, most of the time. We can even cast out demons and perform mighty miracles in Jesus' name only to have Him reject us when we see Him face to face (see Matthew 7:21). This is really important because this is an issue of the *heart*.

Our external actions must flow from a redeemed, born-again, regenerated, renewed heart and you can't fake it 'till you make it! Only God can change our hearts that way. Only true believers; genuine disciples; the real children of God can live like that. True good works, which James talks about in his letter, the kind that glorify God and make a real difference in this world, can only flow from the heart of a genuine believer of Christ. Everything else is dead religious works and it is the stench of religion in the nostrils of a holy God.

Are you a child of God? If God was to say, *"If my people ..."* today, is He talking to you? Do you know that for sure? Are you as convinced of your spiritual standing as you are of your own name? Is there any doubt whatsoever that you are born again and already part of the kingdom of heaven? If there is any doubt, then You need to get that sorted before you do anything else. Do not leave that place until you get your spiritual standing in Christ nailed down and understood in such a conclusive way that you never, ever doubt it again.

I have given you lots of verses and passages to read as you assess what it means to be the people of God, but in some ways, we didn't really need to leave our opening verse in 2 Chronicles 7:14. If I was to delete the first word and read the opening part of this verse I believe we would have a very powerful statement about the true people of God in every age and every place, *"My people, who are called by my name, will humble themselves and pray and seek my face and turn from their wicked ways."*

So here in this one verse an exhortation becomes an affirmation. This makes the verse even more confronting for me. If you haven't done this already then, I want to really encourage you to pray and ask God to reveal your heart over the coming days. Tell God you are not interested in playing church, doing what's expected, while deep down inside nothing is really happening! Get serious. Get real with God. Let His Spirit show you your heart and empower you to surrender and let go, as you let God be God. Then, and only then, will this journey we are taking in this book have the impact we all desire it to have.

CHAPTER FIVE
A Firm Foundation

Let me state very clearly that I believe God has absolutely no time for religion. In fact, as I have said hundreds of times over the last forty years, God hates religion. He hates it with a passion. That may be a new thought for you or a timely reminder – either way, it is true.

Regardless of the few obscure references to religion in the New Testament, I want to assure you that religion as described by all the contemporary definitions which lie in books and journals all over the world today – and religion as it's experienced by so many millions of people who claim to be God's people - is so far removed from what God ordained for us and what God desires, that it may very well be the exact opposite of true Christianity.

The fascinating thing I discovered in my research over many years is that of all the definitions of religion I have found, not one of them contain the word *relationship*. That is very interesting and revealing, because even a quick browse through the Bible will reveal to even the most unenlightened, sin-impaired mind that the Christian faith is ALL about relationships!

From Genesis to Revelation, we have the story of God creating us to be in relationship with Himself and with each other. The whole Bible is about relationships and where they broke down and what God did to fix them and what we are meant to do (and not do) to participate in His global campaign to re-establish close, eternal, intimate relationships with His lost children.

I am not talking about man's relationship to God in some abstract philosophical sense here - that's what religion does; that's what philosophy does. I am talking about man's relationship with God – a personal, one-on-one, intimate communion as it was always meant to be. That concept is foreign to religion and most of the definitions you would find out there and yet relationship is what it's all about with God.

That's what the Bible is about; that's what the Great Commission is about; that's what the Golden Rule is about; that's what the Ten Commandments are about; that's what every teaching and instruction from Jesus and Paul and all the other Biblical writers is about. It's all about RELATIONSHIP and none of it is about religion.

So let me ask the question again I posed earlier. When God refers to, *"My people, who are called by my name …."* who is He speaking about? This is very important to establish before we move on to the challenging words which follow. In one sense God is talking to anyone who wants to listen and respond. But in another sense, I believe that only those who have a personal relationship with God, in Christ, will be able to understand and receive what God is saying today. Let me first tell you who God is <u>not</u> speaking about here:

He is not speaking about those people who just subscribe to the organization of human beings known as the church. The badge of 'Christian' is worn by many people across the world but not all of them experience a real relationship with God.

He is also not speaking about those who try to relate to Him through laws, rules, or commandments. Many people think that if they obey a certain set of God-ordained rules or requirements then they are His people. They lift passages out of context in the Bible and miss the real meaning. Like when Jesus said, *"If you obey my commandments, you will be my disciples."* On the surface that looks like a simple formula of man's good works getting him a place on Jesus' team. When we study the whole chapter, the whole book, and the whole New Testament - we get the big picture and see that this verse means: *"If you are My disciples, then you will obey My commandments."*

What Jesus is saying is, *"If you have a real relationship with Me and are filled with My life, then that life within you, as you submit to it, will produce a natural obedience to all that has been commanded, for it will no longer be you who lives, by Me living in you and through you."*

The fascinating thing is that this verse could have been translated either way and still be true to the meaning in the Greek language. Why we chose to translate it in a way that encourages religion, is another matter - for another book!

God is also not speaking about those who know Him only as the God of Abraham, Jacob, Moses, or David. The God Who related to the men and women of ancient times is a God that none of us can relate to for we were not there. We have some really great stories about God's dealings with His people over the centuries, and they can be incredibly encouraging because they do reveal the character of our God which never changes - but until we have our own stories of our own experience of God right now, then we really have nothing at all that is our own.

He is not even speaking about those who relate to the Jesus of the New Testament - the carpenter who lived and walked the dusty streets of the Middle East. This one is really confronting but it's so true. There is a whole *"WWJD - What would Jesus do?"* industry out there still with bracelets and necklaces and all sorts of reminders. I believe that for many people with this mindset, they are thinking of the bearded, sandaled carpenter who lived in a different time, a different culture and someone they never met and will never meet in the flesh. We cannot ever have a relationship with the man Jesus Who walked this earth.

However, we can – and we should – have a relationship with the crucified, risen, living, reigning Lord Jesus Whom we can relate to and through to the Father by the presence and power of the Holy Spirit. This may seem like semantics, and you may well ask, 'Isn't it the same Jesus?' My answer would be yes and no. In essence it is the same Jesus because that carpenter was also God incarnate. But from a practical point of view as we read the narratives of a man who was locked in time and space and therefore removed from our world totally, it is not *that* Jesus with Whom we have a relationship. The Jesus who walked those dusty streets is an incredibly important historical figure, but that Jesus was only here for a short time. He only ministered here for three years ... did what He had to do and left.

His mission was to reach all of God's lost children – not just the ones at that time and in that place. He was not going to do that in a human body, locked in time. He had a job to do in that body and He did it and got out of there so the Holy Spirit could return and make it all real to all of us across the world.

So, we are greatly encouraged and informed by the stories of the bearded carpenter from Nazareth, but none of those stories can introduce us to the Jesus Who is alive and here right now. The stories of old are useless by themselves and can even be used by the enemy of God to rob us of the current reality of our present relationship with Jesus. The eternal, immortal Son of God was in that human body … but too often we only relate to the man, Jesus and not the risen, living Lord of today with Whom we can walk and talk and relate personally thought His Spirit.

He is also not speaking about those who seek to earn His favour with their obedience and Godly lives. There are countless exhortations in the New Testament for us to live a Godly life and obey the commandments and live in a manner worthy of our calling.

Our obedience does not have any bearing on God's grace and favour upon us.

Obedience is for us, not Him. Obedience closes the door to Satan and releases the fullness and abundance of the life that has been given to us freely in Christ. Obedience is essential if we want to live fruitful, abundant lives and if we want to experience the power and glory and wonder of this relationship which has been given to us freely by God.

However, obedience has no bearing whatsoever on our eternal destiny or our relationship with God from His point of view. Our *experience* of that relationship may be affected through the guilt and shame that Satan will try to inflict on us as we open the door to him; we may *feel like* God is no longer close to us - but in reality, our obedience has no bearing whatsoever on our relationship with God which He secured by the blood of His own Son.

He is also not speaking about Bible scholars who try to relate to Him through their knowledge of the written text of Scripture. This one is hard, and I am treading on dangerous, but important ground here. There are millions of people all over the world who have a relationship with the Bible and not with God. In actual fact, they don't have a relationship at all because you cannot relate to anything, but a person, and the Bible is not a person.

We believe that the Bible was compiled under the inspiration and direction of the Holy Spirit and so we place great authority in this written text - and so we should. If everything was left to man's subjective experience of God and there was no objective reference like the Bible, then the church may have wandered off the track completely many years ago.

However, the Bible is still just a book, and you cannot have a relationship with a book. In fact, I would suggest that 90% of the divisions and tensions in the church over the last 2,000 years have been brought about by people like you and me having the wrong attitude to that book and expecting it do something it was never intended to do and is simply not able to do.

We cannot relate to God through the Bible. God is not the Bible. It is a written book. It doesn't matter how much the Holy Spirit was active when it was written - it is still just words on a page - and a living, personal being cannot live in the pages of a book. Any three-year-old child will tell you that! Yet when I hear how people speak of the Bible; when I see the passionate disputes which arise in interpreting the Bible; when I see the agonising struggles to the point of tears that people have in trying to understand the Bible; I am forced to concede that this book is treated by many as if it were God and they do not seem to have a personal relationship with the real living God about Whom and through Whom this Book was written.

The Bible will tell you about God. The Bible will lead you to God. The Bible will also tell you how to experience that personal relationship with God - but the Bible is not God and knowledge of the Bible is not what makes us God's people.

The devil knows more about the Bible than any Christian on the face of the earth and he uses the Bible and our ignorance of what it was meant to be, to bring pain, confusion and division to God's people every day. Bible knowledge can never and will never equate to a relationship with God.

Just look at the early church and their incredible success in spreading the good news of Jesus Christ across the world. The growth rate of the church in those early days, before the Bible was even compiled, was astounding. Herein lies a warning:

We need to be careful we don't trust a book the early Church didn't have, more than we trust the Holy Spirit they did have!

So, who is God speaking about when He says, *'If my people?'* The Apostle Paul tells us in this amazing passage:

> *"Praise be to the God and Father of our Lord Jesus Christ, who has blessed us in the heavenly realms with every spiritual blessing in Christ. For he chose us in him before the creation of the world to be holy and blameless in his sight. In love he predestined us to be adopted as his sons and daughters through Jesus Christ, in accordance with his pleasure and will - to the praise of his glorious grace, which he has freely given us in the One he loves.*
>
> *In him we have redemption through his blood, the forgiveness of sins, in accordance with the riches of God's grace that he lavished on us with all wisdom and understanding. And he made known to us the mystery of his will according to his good pleasure, which he purposed in Christ, to be put into effect when the times will have reached their fulfilment - to bring all things in heaven and on earth together under one head, even Christ.*
>
> *In him we were also chosen, having been predestined according to the plan of him who works out everything in conformity with the purpose of his will, in order that we, who were the first to hope in Christ, might be for the praise of his glory. And you also were included in Christ when you heard the word of truth, the gospel of your salvation.*

Having believed, you were marked in him with a seal, the promised Holy Spirit, who is a deposit guaranteeing our inheritance until the redemption of those who are God's possession - to the praise of his glory." (Ephesians 1:3-14)

Wow! What a great passage. It goes on and there is so much more in that chapter and the next one. I would really encourage you to read the first two chapters of Ephesians over and over and over again until all the lights go on and the word *grace* is flashing so brightly you cannot see anything else for a while.

You were included in Christ, according to this passage, when you heard the truth about your salvation and believed it. At that point the Holy Spirit of God was released in you to make it all real and introduce you to the risen, reigning, Lord Jesus Christ. *"Having believed ..."* Paul said ... believed what? Believed what he had just finished saying, that's what !

- When we believe that God chose us and adopted us as sons and daughters and lavished His grace upon us in Christ ...

- When we believe that our salvation and our eternal life with God is a free gift with no strings attached ...

- When we believe that nothing we do or don't do could ever save us or cause us to lose our salvation ...

- When we believe that our eternal relationship with God was secured on the cross by Jesus before we were even born ... before we could say yes or no ... before we could sin or obey or serve God in any way...

- When we believe that we have been set wonderfully and totally free by the grace of God ... free to love ... free to serve ... free to hate ... free even to sin ...

Only then. When we believe all that, should we then read on in 2 Chronicles 7:14. For then we truly are the people of God about whom He is speaking these powerful words and giving this powerful promise. In Jesus name, please hear this warning: The spirit of religion is alive and well.

The spirit of Galatians 3:1 is here. Those believers in Galatia had sat through Paul's grace teaching and were set powerfully and wonderfully free as they understood grace in all its truth. Within three years they had lost the plot! They hadn't lost their salvation, that was secure, hey just lost the experience and power of their new relationship with God. They allowed themselves to be deceived by religious spirits who robbed them of their foundational understanding of God's grace. They had, as Paul said in Galatians 5, *"fallen away from grace."*

If you do not understand God's grace; if you do not know how you were saved, when you were saved and by Whom; if you are not rooted and grounded in His love and grace rather than your obedience or disobedience - then the rest of 2 Chronicles 7:14 is going to wipe you out in the worst possible way. If you are not secure in your knowledge and experience of God's grace, then when you get to the exhortations to humble yourself and pray and seek His face and turn from your sin, you are going to hear LAW; you are going to hear JUDGEMENT; you are going to hear CONDEMNATION. Satan will guarantee it.

Based on my many years teaching these truths, I am sure some people may already be struggling with the 'If … then' scenarios in earlier chapters. Without a solid grounding in grace, you will not be able to separate your eternal security and your already-established relationship with God, from the clear exhortation to let that grace be effective in your life. Do you remember this verse? I hope so, because it is foundational to this whole book.

> *"By the grace of God I am what I am, and his grace to me was not without effect. No, I worked harder than all of them - yet not I, but the grace of God that was* with me." *(1 Corinthians 15:10)*

This is an incredibly powerful and wonderfully simple verse – I really encourage you to memorise it. Paul firmly establishes without any doubt, that his salvation; his understanding of God; his ability to discern God's will; his ability to read and interpret the Scriptures; his ability to serve God; his desire to serve God - everything is only there by the grace of God.

Do you know what the word translated *grace* is in the Greek ? It is the word *charis*, which means *gift*. So, Paul states boldly that everything he is; everything he has; everything he achieves; everything he understands; is a free gift from God by His grace.

Then he gets even more profound and says his understanding and acceptance of that free gift, resulted in a changed life. His understanding of grace was deep enough to have a radical and life-changing effect on him, so that he worked harder than anyone in obeying the commands of God and heeding the exhortations to go and make a difference in this world.

Then he adds again, just to make sure we know, that even his hard work was the result of the empowering presence of God in his life.

So don't even try to humble yourself and seek God's face and turn from your sin without a solid, foundational understanding of God's grace in your life. If His empowering presence is not flowing through you; if you are not totally and completely assured of your salvation and your eternal security in Christ; then DO NOT PROCEED BEYOND THIS POINT.

If you do push on regardless, then you will probably only see law, judgement, frustration and self-condemnation and any changes which do occur in you will be generated by the flesh and will bear no long-term fruit. If you do not know the difference between the conviction of the Holy Spirit in the hearts of God's people and the accusation and condemnation of Satan, then you need to stop at this point and seek the Lord until you do.

At first, they may look the same, and that's because conviction and condemnation can both drive you to your knees or flat on your face on the floor. Conviction and condemnation can both impact you emotionally and you may cry out to God under the weight of a heavy heart - but that is most definitely where the similarity ends. One will bring life and the other will bring death. One releases, empowers, and transforms, whilst the other binds us and robs us of all power.

If you understand God's grace and have that firm foundation in your relationship with Him, then the teaching which follows in the chapters to come is going to confront you and convict you and force you to deal with the stuff in your own heart which God will reveal - but you will be empowered to do that by God's grace and you will come out the other end in a far stronger position, deeply convicted and fully empowered to make a real difference and bring this city to Jesus.

If you struggle to understand God's grace and do not have a firm foundation in your relationship with Him, then the teaching which follows in this book will wipe you out (assuming you choose to even keep reading). You will be confused, condemned, powerless and very discouraged. You may not even stay in the church.

Such will be the impact of the truth which awaits you in these pages, if you do not get a firm grasp on the foundation and heart of the gospel of God's amazing grace. Which is why I have already stressed that my first book, *Amazing Grace,* should always be read before this book! It provides the firm foundation upon which all the teaching in this book must rest.

We need to pray, and not stop praying, that each and every one of us will press on and embrace the challenging word which I believe is coming from God across the face of the church. He is shaking up the church and has been for several years.

The river is rising; the days are getting fewer; the harvest time is now approaching. God needs an army of people who know who they are in Christ and who understand God's grace in all its truth and choose to allow that grace to have an effect in changing them and releasing them in repentance, humility, prayer and worship.

When this army takes up their position - on their knees, on their face before God - He will bring the victory, as He sweeps whole cities and nations into His Kingdom of light and life and hope.

CHAPTER SIX
Grace Re-visited

In the last chapter we looked again at what it meant to be the people of God. I stressed in the strongest possible terms that unless we really know who we are in Christ; unless we know the foundation of His grace in our salvation and our sanctification; unless we have a solid understanding of what God has done and what He expects us to do (and not do!) in this partnership, then we should not proceed in our study of 2 Chronicles 7:14.

If we do not know the truth of who we are in Christ, how we are saved and how we are supposed to live out that salvation - then the coming exhortations to humble ourselves, pray, seek His face and turn from our sin will too easily become works of the flesh - things we attempt to do in our own power and strength.

The "if ...then" scenario is most definitely present here, as we saw in earlier chapters, but the critical question is how? If our humility, prayer, worship and repentance are not the fruit of the grace of God (i.e. the empowering presence of God), then they will be short-lived, superficial and unsuccessful in moving the hand of God to do anything at all in our land.

So, we are going to remain camped by the river of God's grace a little while longer before we embark upon the journey through these challenging exhortations. My sincere apologies if you were looking forward to having your pride exposed by the Spirit of God as we look at what humility might mean ... but be patient, your time will come!

We just need to drink some more from the living water of God's grace, mercy, forgiveness and love first. We need a refill of gospel truth before we embark upon the treacherous journey ahead. Unless we have our provisions; unless we are stocked well with a clear understanding of God's grace in all its truth, this will be a very dangerous expedition.

To those who think they know all this and are frustrated because I am not moving on to 'the good stuff.' I feel I must inform you, if that's how you feel, then you do not understand grace yet. **If you think you have had enough teaching on grace, then you have certainly <u>not</u> had enough teaching on grace!** If you have the slightest inclination to 'move on' from grace, then I tell you in Jesus' name, you do not understand grace.

We never 'move on' from grace. Open your heart and receive the truth, for in my experience, those who understand grace, even in part, are the ones whose spirit leaps with affirming joy whenever they hear it our read it. They can never have too much of the blessed message of God's grace. Something supernatural inside them resonates with God's truth so loudly, that they can almost hear it screaming out *"Yes Lord! Yes! This is true … this is God … this is the gospel! Preach it …. tell me the old, old story …. more Lord … more …. I can never get enough of this lifesaving …. life-changing truth … my legalistic heart needs reminding over and over again Lord … tell me the old, old story … again … and again … and again!"*

If that is something like what was happening inside you as you read the previous chapter and as you read this one now, then you are well on the way to understanding God's grace in all its truth. If that is not how you feel, then you need a fresh revelation from God … and you need it today!

I believe that having a solid understanding of the grace of God is essential to living a victorious Christian life. Grace is not 'God's unmerited favour' – as many people have defined it. Grace is the empowering presence of God Himself, available to meet our needs, without any cost to us. Without grace, we are nothing, we have nothing, and we can do nothing! It's that simple.

In fact, everything in the Bible - receiving salvation, being filled with the Holy Spirit, fellowshipping with God, having victory in our daily lives – it is all based upon grace. It is very important that you and I understand that there is nothing that we can do to save ourselves and pay for our sins.

Let's read some Scripture verses – from the Amplified version of the Bible:

> *"There is none righteous (none that meets God's standards), not even one. For all have sinned and continually fall short of the glory of God, and are being justified (declared free of the guilt of sin, made acceptable to God, and granted eternal life) as a gift by His (precious, undeserved) grace, through the redemption (the payment for our sin) which is (provided) in Christ Jesus."* *(Romans 3:10,23-24)*

Therefore, since man could not come to God, God came to man.

> *"In the beginning [before all time] was the Word (Christ), and the Word was with God, and the Word was God Himself and the Word (Christ) became flesh (human, incarnate) and dwelt (tabernacled - fixed His tent of flesh, lived awhile) among us ..."* *(John 1:1,14a)*

Jesus became our substitute, paying the debt we owed at no cost to us. He did this out of His great love, His mercy and His grace.

> *"It is by free grace that you are saved (delivered from judgment and made partakers of Christ's salvation) through your faith. And this [salvation] is not of yourselves [of your own doing, it came not through your own striving], but it is the gift of God; Not because of works [not the fulfilment of the Law's demands], lest any man should boast. [It is not the result of what anyone can possibly do, so no one can pride himself in it or take glory to himself]."* *(Ephesians 2:8-9)*

What you and I could not earn, God gave to us freely by His grace. But His grace affects our lives in so many other areas. We must realize that God's grace is available to us to make all the needed changes in our life. Just as we received our salvation by grace through faith, we need to also trust and receive every other blessing from God in the same way – by His grace. I'm not sure about you, but when I first got saved, I thought all my problems were being caused by someone else, and if only they would change and act differently, then I would finally be happy.

I eventually let the Word of God convict me and reveal that I was the one with the problem. I was the one who needed to change. It seemed like every time I opened the Bible, the message was for me, as stuff in my life that needed addressing kept rearing its head. It wasn't long before the devil took the conviction that God meant for good and turned it into condemnation. I entered into a seemingly endless cycle of trying and failing. The old 'do-more-try-harder' treadmill was operating overtime. All that I knew was to try harder to do what the Word of God said I should do.

It seemed that I was always trying. I tried to be good and operate in the fruit of the Spirit. I tried to pray and read the Bible more. I tried to love those close to me and tried to love those in the world around me. I tried to be a better person in so many ways. I tried and tried and tried until I almost died! All my human efforts produced was more frustration. The word *frustrate* is defined in Webster's dictionary as '*to prevent from obtaining a goal or fulfilling a desire.*' It comes from a Latin word which means *to disappoint*.

Interestingly, Galatians 3:10 says, "*... all who depend on the Law [who are seeking to be justified by obedience to the Law of rituals] are under a curse and doomed to disappointment.*" And that is exactly where I was. I had gotten into the habit of taking every Scripture and every sermon I heard and hearing, "*If I don't do this, God doesn't love me anymore. If I don't do this, I'm going to lose my salvation.*" I was being destroyed inside because I lacked the knowledge of the truth (see Hosea 4:6).

Jesus said that the truth will set us free (John 8:32). Well, the opposite is true too - if you do not possess the truth then you will never be free. You will be in bondage and like so many millions of people in church across the world I was in bondage for many years and didn't want to admit it. I was blinded by unbelief and just could not see the truth.

Then the Lord in His mercy opened my eyes so that I could see what is really in the Bible and that radically changed my life. One of those verses was Galatians 3:3, "*Are you so foolish? After beginning with the Spirit, are you now trying to attain your goal by human effort?*"

God showed me that I was trying in my own strength and effort to live according to His Word. As I did, I was putting myself back under the law and anytime we put ourselves under the law, we are doomed to disappointment and frustration because we will never be able obey the law. That is why Jesus had to come to do it for us! He still wants to do it for us - but we have to get out of the way and let Him!

Why do we always seem to want to do it ourselves? It's because that is the nature of the flesh. The flesh, that is our fallen, sinful nature that we have had from birth, wants to conquer its own problems so it can get the glory.

I used to think that when I was getting frustrated it was because the devil was attacking me. I would rebuke him and do some fancy praying and spiritual warfare; I would 'put on the whole armour of God' in some ritualistic way. You name it - I tried it - but my rebukes always seemed to fall on deaf ears because the devil wasn't my problem.

Then I discovered that it was actually God who was frustrating me. Scripture says, *"God opposes the proud but gives grace to the humble."* (James 4:6). Wow! What revelation that was. Little did I know, while I was doing all that fancy praying and spiritual armour rituals .. it was God Who was coming against me because of my pride. As long as we try to figure things out ourselves, we are being proud.

Instead of working at obeying the Word, we need to let the Word work in us to produce that obedience as a fruit of the life of Jesus in our hearts.

We cannot change ourselves. It is the God of peace Himself that sanctifies us through and through, separating us from profane things and making us pure and wholly, i.e. consecrated to God (1 Thessalonians 5:23).

When you're convicted by the Spirit to change something in your life, don't take on the task yourself.

Just agree with the truth God shows you and say,

> *"Yes, Lord, I need to do that. Your Word is right, and my life is not matching up with the truth that is in my heart. I can see that I'm wrong in this area. I want to change … and by Your grace I will change. I thank You again for the forgiveness that is mine in Christ and I ask that You change me by Your grace."*

In this position of surrender and humility, God gladly gives us more and more grace; His empowering presence; the power of the Holy Spirit released in us, to meet any and every challenge. (James 4:6). Everything we receive from God - from salvation to sanctification - comes to us by grace and through faith. Grace is the power and faith is the channel or instrument it flows through. Both are needed - we can't have one without the other.

Take, for example, an electric fan. On a sweltering hot day in a room with no air conditioning, an electric fan would be an absolute blessing. But if the fan were placed next to you without being plugged into an electrical socket, it would be of no value. It would only torment you! You could have all the fans money could buy, but they wouldn't do any good at all if they were not connected to a power source.

Well, it's the same way in our relationship with God. We could know thousands of methods, principles, and formulas, but have no power to make them work. Prayer, Bible study, worship, obedience, confession, are all good, and we need them. But if we are not plugged into the power source of God's grace, all our methods, channels, programs and disciplines are useless.

The victory is not in our methods - it's in God. It's … *not by might, nor by power, but by My Spirit...says the Lord God* (Zechariah 4:6). God doesn't want us to have faith in faith; He wants us to have faith in Him. He wants us to be connected to Him - spending time with Him in personal, private, intimate fellowship. He wants us to seek His face and not just His favours. He wants us to come into His presence because we love Him and want to be with Him, not just because we have our list of requests.

We are not spending time with God to get or earn His grace. His grace is a free gift – it is never for sale and therefore it cannot be bought with good works – no matter how 'holy' those good works appear. The reason we should all spend time with God is because we love Him. It may seem awkward to you at first - it was for me - but the more time you spend sitting in His presence, the more you will learn to relax and relate to Him as a person.

When God opened my eyes to His grace, I began to understand what He was trying to tell me all along. I began to realize that we are saved by His grace <u>and</u> sanctified by His grace. But I still had this feeling lingering within me that I needed to <u>do</u> something. I can't tell you how many times I cried out to God saying, *"What do You want me to do? If You'll just show me what to do, I'll do it."*

Well, one day God gave me an answer. It was there all the time … I just didn't let it register. He brought me to John 6:28. It's here that the disciples asked Jesus the same question I was asking, *"What must we do to do the works God requires?"* Then in verse 29 Jesus responded, *"The work of God is this: to believe in the one he has sent."* That's the answer. *Believers* are supposed to *believe!* How radical is that?! Isn't that embarrassingly simple? Maybe that's why the Bible calls us *believers.* We are to believe in Jesus, and trust what the Word of God says about our situation more than we trust what we want, think, or feel. It's true that we need to be obedient to what God has told us to do, but we must realize that only God, by His empowering presence (by His grace) can enable us to make the necessary changes in our lives.

All of my life I have been a *thinker.* I always had a *plan* for how to change my family, myself, and others, and I was always trying to figure out how God was going to do it. I am still like that to some extent … God has some more work to do in me yet … but He cut a lot of that out of me when I got smacked in the face with a statement in Proverbs:

> *"Trust in the LORD with all your heart and lean not on your own understanding; in all your ways acknowledge him, and he will make your paths straight." (Proverbs 3:5-6)*

It is still important to have a plan, otherwise we will never get anything done. But we can't put our faith in the plan - we need to put our faith in God.

> *"In his heart a man plans his course, but the LORD determines his steps." (Proverbs 16:9)*

We need to plan, but we have to be very careful that we don't go overboard and get into excess and wear ourselves out. What we need is balance. The moment we get confused, we've gone too far in our planning. When we sense frustration and confusion, we have stopped drinking from the reservoir of God's grace inside us and have slipped into works of the flesh again.

Grace and works are totally opposite to each other. The more we come to understand what grace is, the less we're going to worry and struggle trying to figure everything out. I discovered that as long as I tried to figure out a way to fix myself or my situation, God withheld His help from me. But when I settled down and believed God to show me what to do, He always gave me the answer I needed - when I needed it.

God is never early and never late – He is always right on time. It is by His grace through faith that we are saved, and it's by His grace through faith that we are changed into the likeness of Jesus. Our faith is the channel - His grace is the power. There is a time for specific action, and as we trust God, He will show us what to do and when to do it.

Perhaps God is confronting you now, the way He has continually confronted me over the years. Perhaps He is asking the question He has asked me many times. ***Are you an achiever or a believer?***

Where is your energy and time being directed - achieving or believing? We all want to achieve - and we will, by His grace, through faith. Too often we set out with the best of intentions to achieve, even in His name sometimes, without knowing that this is an act of our fallen flesh, and it will never bear fruit in the Kingdom of God - the kingdom of grace. I challenge you to give up achieving (in the flesh) and start believing!

God is able to do exceedingly and abundantly more than all we could ask or even imagine (Ephesians 3:20) when we *believe* Him and allow His grace to have an effect in us and through us. God can do nothing through unbelief and works of the flesh. In fact, He will actively oppose them all the time because works of the flesh are manifestations of pride and God opposes the proud, but He gives grace (His empowering presence) to the humble.

As you trust God's Word and walk in obedience, God's grace will always be available to meet your every need … then they will be <u>His</u> methods and <u>His</u> plans, and we already know that His plans are always good, don't we? Well, we should:

> *"I know the plans I have for you," declares the LORD, "plans*
> *to prosper you and not to harm you, plans to give you hope*
> *and a future. Then you will call upon me and come and pray to*
> *me, and I will listen to you. You will seek me and find me when*
> *you seek me with all your heart. I will be found by you,"*
> *declares the LORD, "and will bring you back from captivity …"*
> *(Jeremiah 29:11-14)*

That 'captivity' for many people in the church today is the prison of the flesh - the chains of legalism - the bondage of religion and we all know that God hates religion and He loves to break its power in our lives and that's exactly what He will do when we choose to believe God and understand His grace in all its wonderful, life-changing, city transforming truth!

CHAPTER SEVEN
What do you Really Want?

In this chapter I was expecting to start into the really juicy part which deals with humility and therefore that ugly five letter word - pride. However, as I began preparing what will be a few chapters on that one issue, I realised something very important. It was something which I talked about in the opening chapter of this book.

You will remember that I put forward the following formula for success, and by 'success' in this context, I mean us actually seeing God heal our land.

$$\frac{\textbf{Desire + Choice + Commitment}}{\textbf{Prayer}} \quad = \quad \text{SUCCESS}$$

Before we move on in this study, I believe we need to come back to the very beginning and look at that first word in this formula. We talked at length about our choices and the commitment we need to have to see those choices bear fruit and how essential it is to undergird and saturate all this with persistent prayer ... but nothing will happen without *desire*. Until we *really* want God to heal our land, this formula; the teaching in this book; all of our prayer initiatives and every ecumenical program under the sun will amount to nothing.

> *"Man looks at the outward appearance, but the LORD looks at the heart."* (1 Samuel 16:7)

God is never impressed by our prayer meetings or our mission statements or our programs or our Pastors gatherings or our combined churches initiatives or anything else we do. He often blesses those things and encourages us in them, but He is not *impressed* by them. In other words, those things we <u>do</u> are not what moves the heart and the mighty hand of God to revive the church and heal our land.

If, however, those things which we do and participate in are *the fruit of something else;* if they flow from a deep desire in our hearts; a crushing burden in our souls; an agony in our spirit for the lost and lonely and hurting people in our city and our nation; if that deep crushing desire to see God set His children free is what motivates us to pray and do all the ministry stuff, then that is something God can work with!

We therefore need to allow the spirit of God to search our hearts and expose the truth that lies within. We need the light of God's Spirit to shine into the dark corners of our wicked heart and reveal the ugly pride and self-serving motives that can be lurking there, more often than not.

I believe it's entirely possible that many of us who are praying for revival and longing to see our city transformed, do so with wrong motives. This is where pride gets in right at the start. It's so subtle, so insidious and so incredibly damaging to the cause for which we pray. I am sorry if this is a hard word, but I believe that many people who pray for revival and transformation and for God to heal their land, do so for selfish reasons, motivated by corrupt desires. We may want to be part of a revival more than we want to see people set free. We may care more about our reputation and being part of a church that is alive and active and making a difference in the community than we do about the people out there who are trapped in sin and shame and who face each day without hope, without purpose, without joy and without love. It is entirely possible that we are actually focused on a ministry or a movement more than on the people.

Until we get in touch with our real motives, desires and priorities and face the truth of what motivates us to even talk about revival; until we face the possibility that we really do not care all that much about the tens of thousands of people surrounding us each day who live outside the knowledge of God's love and grace and forgiveness; until we deal with our true desires and then ask God to change them if necessary, then there is no point in trying to embrace the teaching in this book or, for that matter, no point in continuing any of our church ministries either!

God is not impressed by any of that. God is not impressed by our worship or our music or our teaching or any of the hundreds of sermons I have preached about revival and transformation over the years. That is all pleasing to God but none of that *impresses* God in the sense of moving His mighty hand to heal this land.

What really impresses God; what moves God; what releases the awesome power of God across whole cities and nations is a broken and contrite heart, humbly bowed before the Lord, crushed by the burden of desire to see God's children set free from the clutches of sin and Satan. If and when the desire of our heart matches the desire of God's heart, and we begin to actually care more about real people than we do about revival and transformation and numbers - then our prayer initiatives and our programs will begin to move the mighty hand of God.

While you and I sit in our Christian fortress each Sunday singing praises to God and asking that He might heal our land – His lost children are being blown apart by sin and Satan. While you and I share the love and mutual support of our brothers and sisters in Christ, people as young as 10 years old are preparing for a night on the streets - devoid of hope, purpose and love.

I believe God is speaking to us every day and challenging our core beliefs and priorities, if only we had the courage to listen and respond. I believe He is saying something like this:

*"I know you care about revival; I know you want to pray for the lost; I know you want to see your city transformed; I know you want Me to heal your land; but there is something I don't know, and until I know this one thing, I cannot answer any of your prayers. I want to know **do you really care about my children?** You are surrounded by My lost children every day – broken and full of pain and agony and the fruit of this fallen, sinful world in which they live. Show Me you care about them as hurting people. Look into their eyes; step into their shoes; sit with them as they cry, as they lash out in pain, as they break apart for lack of love. This is the seed bed of revival. This is where transformation begins. This is the cutting edge of the Kingdom of God. Do you still want Me to heal your land?"*

Until we have God's crushing burden for the people in our city; until we want to see the people in our land set free as much as God does - it will not happen. When we finally get to talk about what *"humbling ourselves"* really means in this verse, we will see that in the first instance it means that as we bow before the Lord in brokenness, contrition, and humble submission, we are then overtaken by His presence, overwhelmed by His broken heart, and consumed by His desires and His passions.

That will release in us a REAL burden for REAL people, and we will stop praying for 'revival' and 'renewal' and 'transformation' and 'healing' and 'restoration' and we will start praying for people by name and we will start moving out of our comfort zone - prepared to be the answer to those prayers.

2 Chronicles 7:14 is a great verse in its original context and as a verse which reveals the heart of God. It has inspired many good sermons and sermon series; it has birthed a few good songs along the way too. But are we prepared to really take the words in this verse seriously? Do we actually think that God can and will heal our land when we, His people, humble ourselves, pray, seek His face and turn from our sin? Do we really believe that is what God's agenda is right now?

Well, let me tell you about a small group of people who decided to take 2 Chronicles 7:14 seriously many years ago. As I share this story, I believe God wants us to listen very carefully for HIS agenda, HIS heart and HIS promise to us and all believers. Like every story, there are specific things which apply to the people concerned at that time, but there are also solid principles which reveal the heart of God for us all and His will for us here and now. It is the latter I believe God will show us here – if we are brave enough to receive it.

In 1949, the Presbytery of the Free Church of Scotland, gathered in Stornoway to discuss the sad state of the church. Dead, dry and without much hope, some of the congregations were ready to close their doors. The young people were in the pubs and the dance halls - they were not at all interested in spiritual things.

As a result of this meeting, seven men and one of the elders decided to pray and seek God for the Hebrides Island. They met in an old barn by the side of the road. Three times a week they met and prayed and sought the face of God. As they humbled themselves and knelt in the straw of the old barn, God reminded them of a verse of scripture. Yes, you guessed it:

> *"If my people who are called by My Name will humble themselves, and pray, and seek My face, and turn from their wicked ways, then will I hear from heaven and forgive their sin and heal their land."*(Chronicles 7:14)

They decided to take this verse seriously for the first time in their lives and treat it as a current promise to them. So, they began to pray according to this verse. The Holy Spirit soon gave them a clear revelation - that God was a covenant-keeping God. As God revealed the "if – then" reality of this verse and His dealing with mankind over so many years, these men came to terms with their responsibility for the condition of their church and their land. They believed that if they were to humble themselves and pray and seek His face and turn from their sin, then God was bound by His own covenant to come and heal their land.

So, they continued to pray day after day - keeping their faith strong and reminding God of His word. They cleansed their hearts; they sought His face and they held on to the covenant promise. They had no doubt that God would heal their land and visit the people of the Hebrides.

At the same time, two elderly ladies, sisters in fact, one was 82 and the other was 84, had also received a similar conviction from God and were also praying continually in their cottage - for God to come in His power and visit their island. One night, after five months, as the men were praying and travailing before God, suddenly the barn was filled with the glory of God. At exactly the same time, the little cottage where the two aging sisters were praying, was also filled with the glory of God - they knew that God had heard them and that He was about to descend in power among them.

The sisters felt convicted that God wanted them to write to Duncan Campbell, a well-known Keswick speaker - a godly man of prayer. God revealed to the sisters that he was the man the Lord was calling to preach during this visitation of the Spirit. Campbell received the letter but replied that his itinerary was full, and that they should continue to pray and that he would come the following year.

When the sisters heard this, they boldly said, "*God is coming in two weeks - not next year!*" They continued to pray even harder and were not surprised at all to learn that Duncan Campbell's itinerary was changed unexpectantly - so he decided to go instead to the Hebrides and be available to preach.

The first night of meetings in the Church at Barvas was relatively uneventful - nothing much happened, but one of the praying deacons said to Duncan Campbell, "*Don't be discouraged, it is coming. I can already hear the sound of heaven's chariot wheels. We will have another night of prayer and then we will see what God is going to do.*"

The meeting finished and about thirty people went to a nearby cottage and continued to pray into that night. At about 3am God swept into the cottage and about a dozen were laid prostrate on the floor, unable to move. Something had happened! Revival had come! As they left the cottage, they found the lights were burning in every house as men and women had been simultaneously touched by the Holy Spirit and we were seeking God. They found men laying by the roadside before the sun had even risen. They were under conviction of sin, crying out for God to have mercy on them.

The events of the second night will never be forgotten by those who were there! Buses came from the four corners of the island. Seven men were being driven to the meeting in a butcher's truck, when suddenly the Spirit fell on them in great conviction - they were all converted before they even reached the meeting! As the preacher spoke, a tremendous conviction swept through the people and tears streamed down the faces of all those present.

So deep was the distress of some that their voices could be heard outside. The meeting finally ended, and people began to move outside. A young man began to pray under a tremendous burden of intercession, He prayed non-stop for 45 minutes and as he prayed people gathered outside the church until there were twice as many outside as there had been inside.

When he stopped praying, an elder read Psalm 132 and as the great congregation began to sing, the people streamed back into the church again and the meeting continued until about 4am. The moment people took their seats the Spirit of God began to sweep through the meeting with great conviction and hardened sinners wept and confessed their sins. As the meeting was closing, a messenger hurried to the preacher, *"Come with me! There's a crowd of people outside the police station; they are weeping and in awful distress. We don't know what's wrong with them, but they are calling for someone to come and pray with them."*

Describing the scene outside the police station the Minister later declared, *"Oh I saw a sight I never thought possible. Something I shall never forget. Under a starlit sky, men and women were kneeling everywhere, by the roadside, outside the cottages, even behind the haystacks, crying for God to have mercy on them!"* Nearly 600 people had been making their way to the church, when suddenly, right outside the Police Station, the Spirit of God had fallen upon them in tremendous conviction, causing them to fall to their knees in repentance.

The revival began to sweep into Arnol, another district where people had been praying and crying out to God because of the deadness of religion. In desperation a little band of men made their way to a farmhouse to plead the promises of God. Just after midnight a young man rose and prayed a bold prayer that will never be forgotten by those present:

"Lord, You made a promise, are you going to fulfil it? We believe that You are a covenant-keeping God. Will you be true to Your covenant? You have said that You will pour waters upon him who is thirsty and floods upon the dry ground.

Lord, I know how these ministers stand in your presence, but if I know my own heart I know where I stand, and I tell Thee now that I am thirsty. Oh, I am thirsty for a manifestation of the presence and power of God! And Lord, before I sit down, I want to tell You that Your honour is at stake here!"

Then came the answer! While the man prayed the house shook like a leaf as God turned loose His mighty power - the dishes rattled on the sideboard. The elder exclaimed, *"It's an earth tremor!"* Wave after wave of divine power swept throughout the farmhouse. Simultaneously, the Spirit of God swept through the entire village. People could no longer sleep; houses were lit all night; many people walked the streets under the conviction of the Spirit; people knelt by their bedsides crying out to God to help them.

As the praying men left the prayer meeting, the preacher walked into a house for a glass of milk. He found the lady of the house, with seven others down upon their knees crying out to God for forgiveness. Within 48 hours, the local hotel, usually crowded with the men of the village, was closed and remained closed. Within 48 hours nearly every young person between the ages of 12 and 20 had surrendered to Christ, and every young man between the ages of 18 and 35 could now be found in the prayer meetings.

This is what can happen when people like us take God seriously and when the words of 2 Chronicles 7:14 are treated as a promise of God to all His people in every age and location! The people who met to pray in that barn were no different to you and me. Those two precious ladies who prayed together in their home were not super saints with special powers - they were just two normal, Godly, Christian women with a genuine desire to see God's people set free.

Do you want that kind of reality to unfold in your city? Notice I didn't ask if you wanted to be part of an exciting revival story … I asked if you wanted the reality behind the story.

Do you want to still be in church at 4am in the morning, weeping on your face before God as His Spirit moves in power? Do you want to have totally unchurched people suddenly appear from nowhere, undone by the power of God, totally ignorant of what church is all about or how to dress or speak or behave? They will just come because God calls them and convicts them. Is that what you really want? If your answer is no, then you had better hope that revival never comes!

Are you prepared to have your comfort zone annihilated so that you may never be comfortable again, in the sense of being in control of what is happening around you and to you and in you?

This is what can happen when the kingdom of darkness gets a revival-sized kick in the teeth from the Kingdom of God. When Jesus said, *"The kingdom of God is forcefully advancing, and forceful men lay hold of it ..."* this is what He saw.

Is this what you signed up for? Is this what church is all about when you think of church at its best? Does this sound a little threatening? Will this upset your predictable, non-threatening, church life a little too much? God is asking these questions - not me - God is asking us all if we *really* want Him to heal our land – His way?

God is in the business of revealing hearts, and as painful as it may be for some of us, He is going to reveal every heart in his church and He will show us what is in there; He will show us how much we really want Him to heal our land; He will reveal our selfishness, our insecurities, our pride, our arrogance, our laziness, our wrong priorities and our greed. It will all come out - not to judge us or condemn us - but to reveal the real barriers to city-wide transformation and nation-wide revival.

All those barriers lie within your heart and mine and God will systematically expose them and give us the power to remove them and press on to see the fulfilment of His plan and purpose in our church, in our city and across our wonderful land.

This may be a rough ride, but a very exciting ride. It will be an uncomfortable ride at times, but it will be God's ride, not ours; God's agenda - not ours and if we are serious about revival; if we genuinely care about His lost children; we will strap ourselves in and get ready for the ride of our life.

The choice is ours: Will it be God's way or our way? Revival or dead religion? A city transformed or a city doomed? A nation on its face in worship before Jesus or a nation slipping faster and faster into total moral decay? The ball is in our court - as it has always been. Are we serious or not?

CHAPTER EIGHT
Pride and Humility – An Overview

We finally come now to the part you've been waiting for - the part that deals with humility and pride. I know how desperate you are to get to this section of 2 Chronicles 7:14 and just to make sure you are not disappointed; I shall be spending several chapters here before moving on!

However, a word of warning first: Satan is real, and the powers of darkness are active whenever the Word of God is preached, written or read – but especially <u>this</u> word! The enemy of God has been waiting patiently for this part of the book because he wants me to teach about pride more than anyone.

Satan is so ready, willing, and more than able to take my words of exhortation and instruction; words which are intended to bring life and light and hope and personal transformation; words which are meant to change us more and more into the image of Jesus; and attach discouragement, doubt, fear, depression, guilt, condemnation and a sense of hopelessness.

That is always Satan's agenda and unless you are aware of his schemes and alert to his plan, you will fall victim to his ministry of darkness so that teaching which is intended to release you will actually bind you; words which should bring you hope will bring you despair. So be warned.

All truth is confrontational - I make no apology for that. When the light of God's Spirit shines into our wicked hearts, it can really sting and make us want to hide as we are confronted with some pretty horrible realities. When the conviction of the Holy Spirit reveals stuff in us that needs dealing with – it is not a pleasant experience in the flesh.

In fact, our fallen flesh will often fight against it, and this can produce a huge struggle within us. Yet in that struggle we must take heart.

When God is at work, there should be absolutely NO guilt, NO condemnation, NO discouragement, NO doubt, and NO fear - because we know that we are saved, redeemed, reconciled, and loved by God; we know that we are forgiven, cleansed, and renewed - absolutely nothing His Spirit dredges up in our heart is going to change that.

When we understand God's grace and our relationship with Him is secure and not based on the purity of our own fallen heart – then we can let God's Spirit expose anything and everything in us without fear. In fact - we should welcome it! We really need to have that stuff exposed and removed so that we can be more effective disciples for Jesus; so that we can be used by Him in mighty ways, without any hindrance or burden.

It is important that the pride and sin in our hearts is revealed for <u>us</u> - not for God. That stuff which we deny and lock away inside is hurting us and attracting the ministry of Satan. He inhabits that pride and sin; it is an open door for him to render us ineffective in our ministry and in our life.

We really should welcome the probing and the pain that sometimes comes when the Spirit of God exposes the truth in our own hearts. It may not be enjoyable, but the outcome is new life, renewed power and positive fruit beyond our imagination.

Through this book, the confronting light of God will be shining brightly, and I know it may hurt our eyes at first - we may even want to turn and run. Sadly, a number of people I have preached this to over the years have done exactly that - and this is Satan's intent. He will do whatever you let him do to prevent you from allowing the transforming work of God in your life.

Satan can do NOTHING other than what you allow. He has <u>no</u> authority over you, other than that which you give him. If you feel discouragement, depression, condemnation, doubt, fear of any kind from anything you read in this book, you need to know that you are not getting that from me; you are not getting that from God; you are listening to Satan and his religious spirits.

The Bible says that we should be transformed by the renewing of our minds (Romans 12:2). What you think will determine how you live, so you need to think the right stuff about God and your life and Satan and the conviction of sin and God's purposes in revealing truth to you.

If you truly understand grace and know the love, mercy and forgiveness of God; if you know that nothing you do or don't do will ever change God's love and grace toward you, then you will be free to have your heart, your motives and your deepest thoughts stripped naked before God without any fear. In fact, you will be as excited as a sick person is when the doctor walks into the room and announces that he has found the problem! At last, your pain will end. So, let's be brave, ok? Pray with me now:

> *Come Holy Spirit … come Great Physician … probe, cut,*
> *examine, expose, reveal all that is in us that does not belong;*
> *all that is in us which is hurting us and rendering us ineffective*
> *in our quest to see this city and this nation embrace the Lord*
> *Jesus. Come and do what you need to do. Give us courage.*
> *Give us faith. Give us courage. Give us strength and*
> *persistence. In Jesus' name we pray, amen.*

Humility is not a popular human trait in the modern world. It's not promoted in the talk shows or celebrated in valedictorian speeches or commended in seminars or listed as a core value in mission statements of large corporations – or most churches for that matter! If you go to the massive self-help section of most libraries or bookshops, you won't find books on humility.

The basic reason for this is simple: **true humility can only thrive in the presence of God.** Where God goes, humility goes. In fact, you might say that humility follows God like a shadow. We can expect to find humility applauded in our society whenever we find God applauded - which means almost never.

The following extract is from an editorial which appeared in a large newspaper some years ago and I think it captured the atmosphere that destroys humility:

"There are some who naively cling to the nostalgic memory of God. The average churchgoer takes a few hours out of the week to experience the sacred ... but the rest of the time, he is immersed in a society that no longer acknowledges God as an omniscient and omnipotent force to be loved and worshiped. Today we are too sophisticated for God. We can stand on our own; we are now prepared and ready to choose and define our own existence."

What a sad, but accurate commentary on life in the 21st Century. In such an atmosphere, humility cannot survive. It disappears along with any concept of God. When God is neglected, the runner up 'god' takes His place, namely, man ... and that, by definition, is the opposite of humility: pride.

So, the very atmosphere we breathe in this fallen world is hostile to humility. I want us to look at some words from the Apostle Peter – words which will seem utterly foreign in our society and life as we know it in this nation in the 21st century - but words which are vitally necessary to hear.

If what is said in this passage doesn't take root in our lives, then I am afraid that effectively speaking, we will not be a Christian church - we will not be salt and light in a perishing world and God will not heal this land through us.

"Young men, in the same way be submissive to those who are older. All of you, clothe yourselves with humility toward one another, because "God opposes the proud but gives grace to the humble." Humble yourselves, therefore, under God's mighty hand, that he may lift you up in due time. Cast all your anxiety on him because he cares for you." (1 Peter 5:5-7)

The main point of this passage is that we Christians should be humble people. The exhortation comes in one form or another three times:

1) Verse 5a: "*Young men, be submissive (i.e., be humble toward) to your elders.*"

2) Verse 5b: "*All of you, clothe yourselves with humility toward one another.*"

3) Verse 6: "*Humble yourselves under the mighty hand of God.*"

So, the main point is plain in these verses: humility is essential in the life of a Christian. It is a defining mark of a true Christian. Peter also gives reasons or incentives - at least four.

1) Verse 5b: "*God opposes the proud.*" Nothing could be worse than to have an infinitely powerful and holy God opposed to you. So don't let pride have its way. More on this later.

2) Verse 5b: "*God gives grace to the humble.*" And nothing could be better than to have an infinitely powerful and wise God treat us graciously. He does that to all of us in many ways, but He especially does that to the humble. The reason is clear: <u>Humility is not a performance of virtue that earns grace. Humility is a confession of emptiness that receives grace</u>. "*Blessed are the poor in spirit (humble), for theirs is the kingdom of Heaven.*" (Matthew 5:3)

3) Verse 6: God will use His mighty hand to exalt the humble: "*Humble yourselves, therefore, under the mighty hand of God, that He may lift you up (or exalt you) at the proper time.*"

4) Verse 7: God will use His mighty hand to care for the humble: "*Cast all your anxiety upon Him, because He cares for you.*"

Be a humble person because, if you are proud, God will stand against you in your pride; but if you are humble, He will give you grace, exalt you in due time and care for you along the way so that you don't have to be anxious. That's the basic message of this text. Now how shall it take root in our minds and hearts and make a powerful difference in the way we live to God's honour? Let me try to make it sink deeper into us by asking two questions: What is pride and humility and what's the connection between humility and not being anxious?

I'll start with the second question. In some translations and in the Greek, there is a definite grammatical connection between verses 6 and 7 and therefore it should read like this:

> *"Humble yourselves, therefore, under God's mighty hand, that He may lift you up in due time, casting all your anxiety on Him because He cares for you."*

It's not really a new sentence. It's actually a subordinate clause. *"Humble yourselves . . . casting your anxieties on him."* Therefore, casting your anxieties on God is an expression of humility. For example, it's like saying,

> *"Eat politely ... chewing with your mouth shut."*
>
> *"Drive carefully ... keeping your eyes open."*
>
> *"Be generous ... inviting someone over for a meal."*
>
> *"Humble yourselves ... casting your anxieties on God."*

One way to be humble is to cast your anxieties on God, which means that one hindrance to casting your anxieties on God has to be pride. That undue worry about your future is a form of pride.

Now there is more to say about that, but to feel the full force of it we need to answer the first question, and then come back to this connection between pride and anxiety.

So, what is pride and humility? I'll try to answer that by firstly sharing ten Biblical observations about pride. And then you just need to assume that the opposite of these ten things is humility.

1. Pride is self-satisfaction

God says to Israel in Hosea 13:4-6, *"I have been the Lord your God since the land of Egypt . . . I cared for you in the wilderness, in the land of drought. As they had their pasture, they became satisfied, and being satisfied, their heart became proud; therefore, they forgot Me."*

2. Pride is self-sufficiency and self-reliance

Moses warns the people of God in Deuteronomy 8:11-17 about what will happen when they have rest in the promised land:

"Beware . . . lest, when you have eaten and are satisfied, and have built good houses and lived in them, and when your herds and your flocks multiply, and your silver and gold multiply . . . then your heart becomes proud, and you forget the Lord your God who brought you out from the land of Egypt . . . [and you] say in your heart, 'My power and the strength of my hand made me this wealth."

God's goodness is turned into self-sufficiency.

3. Pride considers itself above instruction

In Jeremiah 13:9-10 God says to the people of Judah:

"I will destroy the pride of Judah and the great pride of Jerusalem. This wicked people, who refuse to listen to My words, who walk in the stubbornness of their hearts."

Pride stubbornly refuses to be taught the way of God and makes its own wishes the measure of truth.

4. Pride is insubordinate

Psalm 119:21 says, *"You rebuke the arrogant, the cursed who wander from your commandments."*

When the decrees and Word of God are spoken, pride turns away and will not submit. It rejects the right and authority of God to tell us anything.

5. Pride takes credit for what God alone does

One of the most vivid illustrations of this is the case of Nebuchadnezzar, the king of Babylon in Daniel 4:30-32:

[Nebuchadnezzar said], "Is this not Babylon the great, which I myself have built as a royal residence by the might of my power and for the glory of my majesty?" While the word was in the king's mouth, a voice came from heaven, saying, "King Nebuchadnezzar ... sovereignty has been removed from you ... until you recognize that the Most High is ruler over the realm of mankind, and bestows it on whomever He wishes."

Then, after his season of humiliation grazing in the fields like an ox, Nebuchadnezzar is restored and confesses:

"Now I, Nebuchadnezzar, praise, exalt and honour the King of heaven, for all His works are true and His ways just, and He is able to humble those who walk in pride."

6. Pride exalts in being made much of

Jesus indicted the religious leaders in Jerusalem for this in Matthew 23:6.

"And they love the place of honour at banquets, and the chief seats in the synagogues, and respectful greetings in the marketplaces, and being called by men, Rabbi."

7. Pride aspires to the place of God

The story of Herod in Acts 12: 21-23 is one of many we could quote here:

"And on an appointed day Herod, having put on his royal apparel, took his seat on the rostrum and began delivering an address to them. And the people kept crying out, "The voice of a god and not of a man!" And immediately an angel of the Lord struck him because he did not give God the glory, and he was eaten by worms and died."

This one act did not bring the wrath of God on its own - but a whole life devoted to playing God resulted in Herod's demise. Pride can have disastrous effects if not exposed.

8. Pride opposes the very existence of God

"In his pride the wicked man does not seek him; in all his thoughts there is no room for God."(Psalm 10:4)

Pride knows that the simplest solution for its own survival would be that there be no God at all. That would be, as the Nazi's might say, *'The Final Solution'* for the survival of pride. It doesn't come as any surprise then that:

9. Pride refuses to trust in God

Proverbs 28:25 contrasts arrogance and trust: *"An arrogant man stirs up strife, but he who trusts in the Lord will prosper."*

Pride cannot trust God. It sees the posture of trust as too weak - too dependent. Trust calls too much attention to the strength and wisdom of another. Trusting God is the heartbeat of humility, trusting God is the opposite of pride.

When pride keeps us from trusting in God to take care of us there are two possibilities: one is that we feel a false security based on our own imagined power and shrewdness to avert catastrophe. The other is that we realize we cannot guarantee our security, and so we feel anxious and fearful. Either way – pride is at work.

Which brings us to the final trait of pride and the last explanation about the connection between 1 Peter 5:6 and 7.

10. Pride is anxious about the future

In Isaiah 51:12-13 God says to anxious Israel that their problem is pride:

"I, even I, am He who comforts you. Who are you that you are afraid of man who dies, and of the son of man who is made like grass; that you have forgotten the Lord your Maker?"

What a confronting word from God! *Who do you think you are to be afraid?* Sounds strange, doesn't it? But that's how subtle pride is. Pride is the root of our anxiety. Now we can see clearly and feel the force of 1 Peter 5:6-7,

> *"Humble yourselves, therefore, under God's mighty hand,*
> *that he may lift you up in due time."*

How shall you humble yourself? The clear answer comes in the next verse. You humble yourself by:

> *"... casting all your anxiety upon Him, because He cares for you."*

In other words, the most humble thing we can do is trust God with everything in every way. Casting your anxieties on God means trusting the promise that He really cares for you and has the power and the wisdom to put that care to work in the most glorious way.

That kind of trust is the opposite of pride. It's the essence of humility. It's the confidence that the mighty hand of God is not over you to crush you but to care for you just like the promise says. Don't be proud, but cast your anxieties on Him because He will care for you. Whenever your heart starts to be anxious about the future – speak truth to your own heart and say:

> *"Heart, who do you think you are to be afraid of the future and nullify the promise of God? No, heart, I will not exalt myself with anxiety. I will humble myself in peace and joy as I trust this precious and great promise of God - he cares for me."*

I want to encourage you to read this chapter again and study these ten manifestations of pride more closely - seeking God as He attaches some specific issues, attitudes and practices to them from your life at the moment. I will be digging deeper in a future chapter in order to nail down some of those specifics – but I would encourage you not to wait for me - but to make an appointment with the Great Physician this week.

Ask Him to examine you and expose anything and everything which may be in you which will harm you and those around you. Any thoughts, attitudes, feelings, past hurts which you have not let go of, anger, resentment, bitterness, arrogance, and pride … all of it … whatever is in your heart which the enemy of God can use to hinder your spiritual growth and effectiveness. Choose this day to lie on that operating table and trust the One Who knows what to do as He exposes and removes every cancerous thought, attitude and habit which may lie within you.

I want to pray for us now. If you can embrace this prayer, then make it your own and trust God to answer you in the days ahead:

We love You Lord … and we know You love us with an everlasting love. We know You care for us deeply and want the very best for us. We know that Your grace and love and mercy cover us like a blanket, and nothing can change that.

We also know Lord that we continue to sin, though forgiven … We continue to fear, though filled with Your peace … we continue to doubt, though we know You are faithful … we continue to miss the mark, though You have done everything for us in order for us to live an abundant, fruitful life.

So we cry out to You this day and ask that in Your grace and mercy and love, You might take that holy scalpel and cut right through our hearts and reveal every last cell of disease … every presence of the cancer of sin … every molecule that does not belong … all the doubt and fear and anxiety and bitterness and resentment … all of it Lord … and with the skill of the best Surgeon in the universe … remove it all and restore us to full health and wholeness and power and effectiveness.

You will do all the repair work … if we would just humble ourselves and submit to You this day and let You shine Your powerful light into our hearts as You carry out an operation which will have the most amazing and life-changing effect on us. Give us the courage to submit and trust and yield and humble ourselves under Your mighty, but ever-so-gentle hand.

In the matchless and blessed name of Jesus we pray, Amen.

CHAPTER NINE
Pride and Humility – Digging Deeper

As I am sure you know from personal experience, having pride revealed in our hearts by the Holy Spirit is not the most pleasant experience and that revelation is quite a humbling experience. Yet we are being reminded in this teaching that pride is part of the very fibre of our fallen human nature and unless we allow the Spirit access into every dark corner of our heart – revealing hidden motives, attitudes, habits and behaviours - then pride will continue to glorify our flesh; it will continue to put self ahead of God, causing us to miss the mark and fail to fulfil our calling and our purpose in God.

Even worse than that, we may find God Himself standing against us, opposing us and resisting us in our pride because as the Scripture reminds us: *God opposes the proud but gives grace to the humble.* I remember these confronting words from a Dennis Jernigan song many years ago:

> *Oh, my children, don't you see - if you live your life like you need me - then all the pain, I would use to build you; and all the pain, I would use to fulfil your heart - for don't you see - I am the answer? I am all you'll ever need. - I am the answer to the life you live. I am all you'll ever need. - live your life like you need me. Children, just live your life like you need me.*

That's a very powerful reminder of the need for us to humble ourselves before God. You may have heard it said more than once, **we don't need God until we <u>need</u> God.** There's a very interesting thing that happens when you need someone - when you *really* need someone. Think about it. It's just not possible to need someone, to express that need and receive from that person, without humbling yourself. When you finally admit that you really need someone other than yourself, for any reason at all, at that point of need - and certainly at the point of receiving from that person - you must humble yourself.

You cannot exalt yourself and express a sincere need of someone else at the same time. You are either lying to yourself and to them and you don't need anyone, or you are shooting yourself in the foot as you desperately try to receive from that person without humbling yourself. It's just can't happen.

As I have shared this earthly pilgrimage with many thousands of brothers and sisters in Christ, I have observed in the vast majority of them at least one time in their lives when they were forced to admit that they really needed God. One of the many tasks of the Holy Spirit is to bring us all to that point, not just once, but many, many times throughout our lives. **Until we experience a deep, gut-wrenching need of God, we will remain strangers to true humility.**

The Holy Spirit is always slowly, systematically moving within us, particularly those in leadership, uprooting things in our lives which have been entrenched and part of our whole being. As the Spirit is given permission to work within us, things that were once solid become fluid; things we thought we had worked out, we are not so sure about now; where there was once dry, firm, solid, predictable ground to stand upon, we now find ourselves floating in the river of God's kingdom purposes and the scenery is changing faster than we would really like. It's breath-taking for some and downright unsettling for others and we don't like to be unsettled, do we?

That prompts a question: who told us that we are supposed to be 'settled' in the first place? To settle down means to grow roots in one place and not to move. When we settle in one place in our life's journey, we can 'set up house' and organise everything and put this over there and that over here. Everything then becomes familiar; routines develop; life becomes predicable; we feel at home; settled; comfortable and in control. By and large, we determine what each day brings.

On one level that sounds very appealing to us. In that kind of scenario, we are the king or queen of our own little empire. We are the ruler of our life and the master of our destiny.

We call all the shots and after a while we get really good at it and we don't seem to need anyone. We especially don't need God, though we may still sing songs and utter prayers which indicate we need Him, the way we live says something entirely different.

That self-sufficient, flesh-dominated, prideful control of our lives is not regarded in a bad light in our world or even in many parts of the Church for that matter. In the earthly realm, such 'settled' people are the confident ones who end up being leaders and they are the ones whom we think 'have it all together.' The rest of the people - the ones who lack that confidence and trip and fall and fail and wonder what life is all about - they are seen as the losers; the ones who can never make it on their own; the ones who just haven't got what it takes.

The truth is, such people *are* the losers, they are the ones who can't make it on their own and haven't got what it takes – and that's the whole point! Enter: the gospel of God's amazing grace which transforms losers into winners and ... wait for it ... it transforms winners (in the flesh) into losers!

In actual fact, we are all losers and none of us have what it takes and none of us can make it on our own. The only difference is some of us know that and some of us don't. Some of us are still deluded and blind, thinking that we can live without needing others and without really needing God. Whereas others have come to the realisation that without others and without God we will not survive very well, and we will never come close to our God-given potential in this life. That illusive reality called *'The Abundant Christian Life'* will continue to be a concept, an out-of-reach goal, or even a myth to so many people! But when the revelation of the Spirit comes - so does humility.

I have listened to people across the church for many years talking and praying about humility and pride. But I also hear people expressing 'wishes' more than prayers, longing for the kind of humility that will attract the real presence of God into our lives, our church and our city.

God understands our current plight. He understands our heart's cry for humility. God will respond and answer us and speak life and truth into us. He will give us the tools we need to take this journey down the river. If we just listen to Him, learn from Him and trust Him with our whole life. Hear the Word of the Lord now; listen to your God; hear what I believe He wants to say to us all right now, today and every day:

"Precious child .... much loved son / daughter ... I am here ... and I know your heart. You are concerned about being humble because you know that I will draw near to the humble and pour out grace and power upon them. You want to be clothed in humility, but you are not sure you know how. You know it represents the opposite of religion and works and pride, and that it's not something you can obtain by striving. So, how, you wonder, do you get it? How do you get this quality that is so vital if you want Me to abide in your midst?

Listen, precious child ... turn your ear to Me today and listen. I say to you, I will open the door to humility to those who ask. Ask Me to help you humble yourself and I will bring circumstances and give you certain keys so that you will know true humility, as my dearly beloved Son knew humility when we walked among you long ago.

I will begin by showing you who I really am - that alone will humble your heart. For My mercy, when truly received, will humble and overwhelm the heart of a person. I will supply grace for all situations, unfailing love, ongoing forgiveness, lack of partiality in every case. As I reveal Myself to you, humility will follow that revelation - if you embrace it.

But what else? I will also reveal to you more about your own nature. For I will give you eyes to see your own inadequacy and the total futility of all human effort. This will be painful at times because one always tends to think, 'I should have done better. I should have been more Christ-like. How could I have acted in such a way?' But I will begin to shatter such illusions of human ability and show you that you, and all people on this earth, are capable of very little. As I reveal this truth, you will not be brought low in condemnation but set free from all self-condemning thoughts.

Certainly, you will still want to be more Christ-like, but you will not be so surprised when you are not. You will only be surprised by My grace and My undying faithfulness to you – as the undeserving, rebellious sinner you are. I will give you clear eyes to see Me and to see yourself. For that is a mark of the humble person - an absence of all misconception.

Did not Jesus say to the Pharisees, "... because you say, we would not have killed the prophets, you indicate by your very words that you would have done so? For you inaccurately think that you are somehow different, better than other men. You inaccurately believe that in you resides some basic good or superior knowledge. Yet this is not so."

Look at those in the Bible who walked in humility. Many of them did not begin on a humble path but, because of My great love for them, I brought them to it. Look at Peter, for his letter clearly speaks about humility. Perhaps he is the clearest of all. He exhorts the pilgrims of the dispersion to be clothed in humility. Had they not been humbled enough by being scattered abroad for their faith?

Yet even to such as these, he urged further humility. 'You humble yourselves and God will lift you up.' This was a man who had been humbled himself and who knew it was the only road to take. Look for other examples of humility - in the Bible and all around you. For if you desire to be humble, I will show you how. I will clearly show you through the life of Jesus and many men and women of faith.

I long for you to understand humility. You may have mistaken it for other things. Humility is not self-abasement or refusal to accept praise. It is not setting yourself apart in an isolated place where you have no opportunity to receive recognition.

For I say, you can walk before all men in humility, you can even receive praise for your deeds and still have a humble heart. My own dear Son, your Saviour, received the praise of thousands on Palm Sunday ... yet the humble state of His heart was clearly revealed a week later when He allowed those worshippers to then become His murderers. Follow Him, learn from Him. That's the humility I seek."

Humility is found as often in the well-known as the unknown. It is found as often in the leader as the follower. It has nothing to do with position or standing. It is an attitude of the heart. Are you surprised by recognition, unaffected by it, unmotivated by it? These are the traits of the humble person. For the humble person is not focused on their own reputation, but on God's. Any credit they receive is a mere sidelight to the main story, the featured event, which is the glory of God filling the earth.

Everything revolves around God and His preferences. This, in turn leads to putting others first. What is in the best interest of my brother or sister? How can I promote him? How can I bless her? How can I help others to succeed … and ultimately, how can I lay down my life for them?

The humble person knows that their life is in God's hands and that He will have His way. We need only to serve God with diligence, doing the work put before us. We are called to do whatever job God gives us, wholeheartedly.

Then, when God so chooses, He will raise us up to a more exalted place. As we put others first, take the lowly job – we will be exalted in due time. God's hand will raise us to a much higher place than we could ever raise ourselves. God's hand will raise us to the place where we were meant to be, the place where we were created to be.

Do you want to be assured of the perfect place for yourself - the place fitted just for you? Do you want to be in the right place at the right time doing the right thing for the right reasons? The place which best utilizes your gifts and talents … the place where you will be enabled to give the greatest glory to your God? Then submit yourself to the hand of God and ask Him to show you the way of humility. Remember the words of Jesus and Peter:

> "Take my yoke upon you and learn from me, for I am gentle and humble in heart, and you will find rest for your souls. For my yoke is easy and my burden is light." (Matthew 11:29-30)

"All of you, clothe yourselves with humility toward one another, because I oppose the proud, but I give grace to the humble. Humble yourselves, therefore, under (My) mighty hand, that (I) may lift you up in due time." (1 Peter 5:5-6)

I am coming to realise more and more that humility and faith are more closely allied in Scripture than we might think. We see it in the life of Christ. There are two cases in which He spoke of a great faith. In the first instance - in Matthew 8:8,10 - the centurion said, *"I am not worthy that you should come under my roof."* At this humility, Jesus marvelled and replied, *"I have not found so great faith, no, not in all Israel."* In the second case - in Matthew 15:27-28 - the mother humbly spoke, *"Lord even the dogs eat the crumbs from the master's table."* And the Lord answered, *"O woman, great is your faith!"*

It is the humility that brings a soul to be nothing before God that also removes every hindrance to faith. Humility makes the soul fear that it would dishonour Him by not trusting Him wholly.

Surely this is the cause of our failure in our pursuit of holiness. Isn't it this which often makes our consecration and our faith so superficial and so short-lived? The eyes of our heart must be opened by the Holy Spirit so we can know the truth about us and God … as painful as that revelation might be sometimes … we *have* to know the truth.

So, what is God revealing? What can we expect if we submit to His Spirit and yield to this powerful move in our midst? Let me suggest what will happen if we allow God to have His way in us.

- We will start to understand to what extent pride and self are still secretly working within us.
- We will see how God alone, by His indwelling Spirit and His mighty power, can cast them out.
- We will start to understand that nothing but a new, divine nature, entirely taking the place of the old self, could make us really humble.

- We will learn that absolute, unceasing, universal humility must be the foundation of every prayer and every approach to God, as well as every dealing with people around us.

- We will realize that we might as well attempt to see without eyes, or live without breath, as believe or draw near to God or rest in His love, without an all-prevailing humility and lowliness of heart.

It is too easy to make the mistake of trying so hard to believe, while all the time our old self in its pride is seeking to possess God's blessing and riches. No wonder we cannot believe.

We need to change our course. IF we seek first of all to humble ourselves under the mighty hand of God, THEN He will exalt us in His time and in His way. The cross, the death, and the grave, into which Jesus humbled Himself, were His path to the glory of God - and they are our path also. Let our one desire and our fervent prayer be: to be humbled with Jesus and like Jesus. Let us gladly accept whatever will humble us before God and men, for this alone is the path to the glory of God.

For those of us who live under the western worldview which is built upon pride, hard work and human achievement, it is really hard to appreciate the fact that there is such an awesome power in humility. Humility seems so contrary to greatness from a western Greco/Roman point of view and yet humility is the key to the fullness, wonder, majesty, and power of the kingdom of God and all its riches and glory.

If we truly want more power and influence with God and with people, then humility should be our greatest desire. If we let Him, God will reveal specific areas in our lives which need our attention, but first and foremost, we need to come to terms with the truth of what I believe God has said in this chapter. We need to get the point where we are finally ready to accept that humility is essential, not just desirable, if we are to live an abundant, fruitful Christian life and touch the pain and loneliness across our city and our nation.

When God sees that we are serious about humility; when God realises that we are willing to be humbled, no matter how that happens; when there is no turning back for us and God knows that. Then, and only then, will we be ready for the next leg of this journey as He takes us one step closer to the day when our whole city and our nation are on their knees confessing Jesus as Lord.

Do you want to see that day? Do you believe that is God's will? Well, the great news is this: community-wide and nation-wide transformation begins right here with you and me - today - as we grapple with this foundational truth concerning humility. I don't say that lightly. I believe I say that with the authority of God today.

The choices you and I make in response to this teaching will have a direct bearing on many thousands of people embracing their salvation in Christ. That's how important this is. That's how urgent the need is. That's how desperate God is to bring His lost children home.

CHAPTER TEN
Pride and Humility – Deeper Still

*"If my people, who are called by my name, will **humble themselves** and pray and seek my face and turn from their wicked ways, then will I hear from heaven and will forgive their sin and will heal their land."(2 Chronicles 7:14)*

It's no accident that the first thing God asks of us in this verse is to humble ourselves. This is the entrance point to the rest of this powerful verse. Once we have clearly established to whom God is speaking (those who are called by His name) we then are faced with this locked door. It is the doorway to the outcome of this verse, which is, God healing our land. The key to that door is humility - no other key will unlock it. We can run around all we like trying to find another way in; we can explore every option we can think of in our foolishness, arrogance, and pride; but we cannot get off the starting line without this one key; we cannot proceed past this point without humility.

I believe the intentional, deliberate structure of this promise from God shows us a truth that is played out on every page of the Bible and throughout all human history. Without humility – we can't even begin this journey! By all means, try if you wish and see what happens. What comes after *humble themselves?* "Pray ..." Well, try having an effective prayer life without humility - it won't happen. Keep going: try *seeking God's face* without humility - it won't happen! Your worship will be man-centred, shallow, and powerless. Try *turning from your sin* without humility – forget it. You may not even see it as sin without humility! Try experiencing the reality and the release of true forgiveness without humility – it will not happen! Can you see why humility is the key to this door?

So how do we get this key? How do we obtain humility? Well, some experts would suggest that we can't. They would say that humility is not something we 'get' as much as it's something that emerges as we deal pride.

We know that pride is the opposite of humility and so as we allow the Lord to reveal pride in our attitudes, thoughts, words, and actions and then deal ruthlessly with that pride by changing what we think and how we live, then we will find that humility is the result.

This view would liken humility to modern medicine's definition of health. Modern medicine would define health as 'the absence of disease' and that is why billions of dollars a day is being spent across the world to help us identify and fight disease. When we get rid of disease in our body – the result is health. So, according to this view, you don't set your sights on this illusive thing called 'health' … rather you set your sights on the enemies of health – germs, bacteria, and the diseases they bring. Get rid of them and you have the absence of disease, which is health.

So, if such a view was applied to our quest for humility, then that would mean we should not set our sights on this illusive thing called 'humility' but rather, we must set our sights on the enemy of humility which is pride. Therefore, the strategy for getting the key to life in this case; the way we arrive at this destination called 'humility' is to clearly identify every manifestation of the vile 'disease' of pride and get rid of it - then the result is humility.

How does that sound so far? Well, just hold that thought for a minute as we consider an alternative viewpoint. Let's jump back for a moment to our example of medicine and the pursuit of health. There is an alternative view to the modern medical view which strongly advocates for preventative methods of achieving health. With this approach, we do focus on health, not disease. We intentionally 'build' health by eating the right foods, getting the right exercise, supplementing our diet with natural herbal products and vitamins and minerals etc.

This view claims that germs do not cause disease - they only seek their natural habitat, which is diseased or weakened tissue in our bodies. Therefore, if we are strong and healthy and fit and our immune system is working well, then we can enjoy a life which is substantially free from all disease.

So, applying this view to our current issue of humility, we would say that humility is to be our focus and we should draw near to God and read His Word and pray and worship and soak up good teaching and do everything we can to attract His real presence in our lives and then pride will have no entry point in such a surrendered, humble heart.

Two very interesting views - but which one is right? I believe they are both valid, and both need to be embraced. I believe the Bible actually gives us a mandate to do both. On the one hand, we are told to draw near to God and focus on the positive. *"Abide in me and I will abide in you."* Hundreds of verses support this view. The closer we get to God; the more we are in His presence; the more we will see His character emerging in us. We become like those we hang around with most. So, hang around with Jesus long enough and His humility is bound to emerge in you.

On the other hand, we are exhorted in the Bible to deal ruthlessly with pride and the many sins which flow from pride. We must allow the Holy Spirit to bring conviction of that sin in our hearts so we can repent. That is, once a particular manifestation of pride is identified, we are meant to turn and walk the other way. That is, we make different choices in the way we think, speak and act so that these manifestations of pride in our lives can be targeted and removed.

So, let's begin with the not so pleasant stuff first, shall we? Let's open the mirror of God's Word and allow Him to reveal our heart and identify some of the many different manifestations of pride. In chapter eight I listed several manifestations of pride. I want us to now work our way through that list in more detail, giving the Spirit of God permission to show us actual attitudes and actions which exist our lives now and should be addressed.

I want to encourage you to get personal and practical at this point. By all means, read through the chapters first, but then make the commitment to go back and work your way through what I have written and write down some any manifestations of pride in your life as the Spirit of God reveals them.

1. Pride is self-satisfaction

> *"I have been the Lord your God ever since you came out of Egypt.*
> *You shall acknowledge no God but me, no Saviour except me. I*
> *cared for you in the wilderness, in the land of burning heat. When*
> *I fed them, they were satisfied; when they were satisfied, they*
> *became proud; then they forgot me." (Hosea 13:4-6)*

Pride and 'self' are inseparably linked. Pride glorifies our fallen human nature i.e. 'self', or 'the flesh' as the Bible calls it. So, it is not surprising to see the term 'self' included in any description of pride. Self-satisfaction always fuels pride.

'Looking after No. 1' they call it. That statement alone is very revealing. The fact that we would even colloquially refer to ourselves as 'No. 1' identifies the root of this prideful attitude.

When we think, even briefly, that we are No.1, then everyone around us, including God, gets relegated to second place and lower. *Our* satisfaction, *our* comfort, *our* needs become primary. Choices we make are made on the basis of what serves <u>us</u>, not others or God. Some of these can be little choices like what will I do tonight? Through to choosing a church fellowship or a career or a husband or wife. Be they small or large choices, we face them all the time, all through our life, and at each point we have an opportunity to do what will serve our needs or what will serve others and God.

We can become satisfied with ourselves as we are and pride will grip our hearts and affect, if not direct all our choices and, as that reading from Hosea reminds us, the result is that we forget God. So, this week, take some time to let the Holy Spirit reveal specific areas in your life where self-satisfaction has become a problem. Write them down, confess them, and ask for God's enabling power as you make different choices in the days ahead.

2. Pride is self-sufficiency and self-reliance

Moses warns the people of God about what will happen when they have rest in the promised land:

"Beware ... lest, when you have eaten and are satisfied, and have built good houses and lived in them, and when your herds and your flocks multiply, and your silver and gold multiply ... then your heart becomes proud, and you forget the Lord your God who brought you out from the land of Egypt ... [and you] say in your heart, 'My power and the strength of my hand made me this wealth." (Deuteronomy 8:11-17)

God's goodness can be turned into self-sufficiency. It is so easy for our prideful human heart to grow out of needing God. The world, our fallen flesh and the enemy of God will convince us to think that we are growing up and maturing and so we can stand on our own two feet now and we don't need a crutch. Therefore, in effect, we don't need God.

When we were little children, we desperately wanted to do stuff by ourselves didn't we? Learning to tie our shoelaces is a classic example. We struggle and try and keep getting it wrong and a parent offers to help, and we protest, *"No! I can do it!"*

Sadly, many of us reach our adulthood still protesting, in so many areas of our lives, *"I can do it!* Much of what we do is done in the power of our fallen flesh, without really relying on God. We insist on doing it our way. Of course, in many areas we can do it without any direct intervention from God. That's how He made us, and He expects that we will grow up and mature and do things ourselves that He once did for us. However, at no point should we ever forget those words of Paul we have read many times now:

"By the grace of God I am what I am, and his grace to me was not without effect. No, I worked harder than all of them - yet not I, but the grace of God that was with me." (1 Corinthians 15:10)

Everything I am and ever hope to be, is only mine, by the grace of God. Everything I achieve that is worthwhile and good is done through the power of God's grace working in me. The moment I forget that, even for a second, I become arrogant and proud and start relying on myself rob God of His glory.

That stubborn, childish insistence which continually says, *"I can do it!"* needs to be broken in us until we begin saying, *"I can do it ... by the grace of God."* That takes humility; that takes surrender and submission and honesty and vulnerability and none of those things will be present when pride is present.

So, take some time and let the Holy Spirit reveal specific areas in your life where self-sufficiency and self-reliance have become a problem. Write them down, confess them, and ask for God's enabling power as you make different choices in the days ahead.

3. Pride considers itself above instruction

> *"I will destroy the pride of Judah and the great pride of Jerusalem. This wicked people, who refuse to listen to My words, who walk in the stubbornness of their hearts." (Jeremiah 13:9-10)*

These are strong words from Jeremiah, but they are so true - then and even more so now. Our fallen, sinful, rebellious nature fights against instruction. Pride stubbornly refuses to be taught the way of God and makes its own wishes the measure of truth. A teachable spirit is a rare and precious gem in a human being and something that God uses so powerfully when He finds such a spirit in a believer.

I would love to say that every Christian I've met has a teachable spirit, but I can't. A teachable spirit does not come automatically with the package of salvation. Like most character traits, it is primarily a choice we must make – every day. There are many people who choose to not keep learning. They arrive at a certain viewpoint, and they camp there, refusing to move.

I know many notable leaders in the Christian Church today, many of whom are scholars with great intelligence and wisdom. Too many of them have taken a black & white, dogmatic stand on some issue which is grey at best in the Bible, and they argue that point with their last breath and refuse to be open to the possibility that they may be wrong. They have set themselves above instruction. They no longer have a teachable spirit.

This does not only apply to academics, prominent Bible teachers and those who have spent years in higher education, although I do think they are more susceptible to this kind of intellectual pride. The more we learn, the higher the risk that we will one day begin to rest on that knowledge and not the grace of God. However, even uneducated people can manifest this kind of arrogance and pride as they refuse to be told anything or accept a different view to their own.

I have always tried to remain open to new information and new insights of truth. Some of the struggles I have with some brothers and sisters in the church are caused by me not taking a definitive stand on certain issues and remaining open to differing points of view - not coming down hard on one side of the fence or the other. There is a price we pay for having a teachable spirit, but I see no alternative, if we are to truly walk in humility.

I want to strongly encourage you to be ruthless in dealing with pride in your heart because it will stop you from learning. The moment you think you are above instruction on any issue … any issue at all … you have hit a major ditch on the side of the road to an abundant, effective, powerful Christian life. A teachable spirit is a sure sign of humility, and it is essential if we are to travel far in our desire to see God heal land. I remember a statement coming from my father's lips when he was with us - a statement I have never forgotten. He said, *"It's what you learn after you know it all that really counts."*

So, take some time this week to let the Holy Spirit reveal specific areas in your life where you may be considering yourself 'above instruction.' Write them down, confess them, and ask for God's enabling power as you make different choices in the days ahead.

4. Pride is insubordinate

When the decrees and Word of God are spoken, pride forces us to turn away and not submit. It rejects the right and authority of God to tell us anything. Now you might be thinking at this point that you are OK in this department.

Perhaps you can't think of any areas where you reject the Word of God and refuse to listen to Him. However, I am not just talking about those who boldly look God in the face, put their hands on their hips, stomp their feet and say *"No! I will not do what You ask."* That kind of bold (but refreshingly honest) insubordination is not how most of us operate. We are more subtle. We just ignore God's Word. We just turn our backs and pretend we didn't hear Him speak, and conveniently forget what God has already said.

God's decrees, God's instructions for daily living; the Father's heart-cry and His will, have all been declared, proclaimed, and shouted from the mountain tops for centuries. Every one of us has more than one Bible in our homes - a Book which, under the influence of the Holy Spirit, contains the instructions of God to His children. It doesn't contain all that God ever spoke or will speak, but it does contain more than enough to reveal His clear purpose for you and for me in this life.

We are without excuse when we lose our way, because God has already illuminated the path for us. When we slip and fall or find ourselves groping in the darkness and cutting our way through the thorny bushes – more often than not, it's because we refused to listen to God and chose to do it our way. We simply didn't follow the instructions. We ignored God. We made deliberate choices to do it our way and there are consequences attached to those choices for which we can blame nobody but ourselves.

We can cry out, *"the devil made me do it"* all we like; we can even try the old line, *"God is testing me at the moment through this trial and tribulation."* Or jut revert to my all-time favourite: *"I am under spiritual attack."* I want to be so bold as to suggest that 99% of the time we are in that ditch, it's because we refused to listen to God. We can soften it a little and call it 'ignoring the clear advice of a loving Father,' or we can call it what the Bible calls it: *disobedience.* Either way, it doesn't really matter, we are just reaping what we sowed, and we need to face that confronting, simple truth and get back on the path God has laid out for us. Go through the Bible and highlight the hundreds of *"If...then"* statements and see how embarrassingly clear God's instructions are.

We encounter horrible stuff in our life; things aren't working out; God doesn't appear to be real; our prayers aren't getting answered the way we want; so, we look to blame our spouse, or our family, or our boss at work, or the church, or the Pastor, or Satan or even God Himself … all the time, making sure we don't go anywhere near a mirror - when in fact that's the very first place we should go for answers!

Before you even pray; before you bother God with your woes; look in the mirror of God's Word; examine your own heart and life and choices and more often than not you will find that you have been insubordinate, disobedient; you've chosen to think, speak or act in a way that is contrary to the clear, fool-proof, guaranteed-to-work-every time clear instruction of Scripture.

5. Pride takes credit for what God does

There are so many examples I could draw from in Scripture to demonstrate this manifestation of pride, but one of the most vivid is the case of Nebuchadnezzar, the king of Babylon:

> [Nebuchadnezzar said] "Is not this the great Babylon I have built as the royal residence, by my mighty power and for the glory of my majesty?" Even as the words were on his lips, a voice came from heaven, "This is what is decreed for you, King Nebuchadnezzar: Your royal authority has been taken from you. You will be driven away from people and will live with the wild animals; you will eat grass like the ox. Seven times will pass by for you until you acknowledge that the Most High is sovereign over all kingdoms on earth and gives them to anyone he wishes." (Daniel 4:30-32)

Then, after his season of humiliation grazing in the fields like an ox, Nebuchadnezzar is restored and confesses:

> "Now I, Nebuchadnezzar, praise and exalt and glorify the King of heaven, because everything he does is right, and all his ways are just. And those who walk in pride he is able to humble." (Daniel 4:37)

This is one of many passages in the Bible and many stories of life in general which demonstrate one ugly manifestation of pride which can be found in almost every human heart. When we take credit for what God has done, we rob Him of His glory, we rob ourselves of His true power and we place the focus back on man's ability and not God's.

The worst part about this is that it can be so subtle and often camouflaged. The vast majority of the time we are not aware that we are even doing this until some brave person, led by the Spirit, points it out to us.

In the case of King Nebuchadnezzar, it was pretty blatant, but I am sure it didn't start that way. This form of pride can start in small, almost invisible ways and the story of Nebuchadnezzar is a reminder of how bad it will become if we don't catch it early and nip it in the bud.

One of the most common examples of this characteristic is evident in how we deal with prayer and God's answer to prayer. This is hard because we must acknowledge that there is most definitely a partnership in prayer - we do have a role to play in the process of prayer - and yet when I hear some people talking about what God has done, in answer to prayer, far too often the focus seems to shift to them rather than God. It is often subtle, almost always unintentional, but all too common. It is also a powerful tool in Satan's hands to deceive us and rob God of the glory due His name.

Let me share two pictures with you. They are vivid extremes, and I stress that. This is not a black and white issue - there are many shades of grey here and we need to work out in our own heart where we stand. But these extremes will highlight the problem.

Scene One: We see a well-dressed business Executive standing outside the office of a wealthy and incredibly powerful man. This Executive is here to put a proposal to this wealthy man in an attempt to persuade him to part with some of his money for a worthy cause.

This Executive is polished, prepared, dressed in his brand new suit, new shoes, a briefcase full of research papers in his hand - the fruit of his training and learning. He has all the goods; he has all the technique; he knows all of the principles; his job is to negotiate with this man - the one who has all the money. That is an important point. This Executive has nothing, in reality. The man on the other side of the door is the one with all the resources. So, the Executive plans to use his skills and his training to secure some of those resources for himself. The door opens, he enters and the negotiation proceeds.

Sometime later the Executive emerges, a huge smile on his face, obviously very pleased with himself and walking slightly taller than before. He winks at the receptionist as he heads for the front door and says smugly, *"I did it!"* There were no comments about the generosity of the man behind the door; no recognition that he could just as easily have rejected his proposal; no concept at all that it was an act of grace even to be given an appointment in the first place!

The Executive heads back to his own office, boldly enters the door shouting to his colleagues, *"I did it; I got the money; my plan worked; my strategies were perfect; all that training paid off; I followed the principles of negotiation perfectly and … I did it!"*

Scene Two: We see a man hanging over a cliff by a rope. He has tied a knot in the end, and he is holding on with all his might. He is helpless; the only way out is down and that's not a pleasant thought. In his own strength he can only just hold on. All he can do is cry out for help and believe that he will be rescued.

He therefore uses all the energy left in his tired body to call for help, over and over again, trusting that someone will hear him. Finally, someone does. A man reaches over the cliff and says, *"Hang on … I've got you; I won't let you fall."* He pulls the man to safety. Now this man who was hanging on for his life is just so overwhelmed with gratitude, he cannot believe that someone heard his feeble cry! He heaps praise and thanks and gratitude upon this saviour who rescued him.

When *this* man arrives home, he doesn't boast about how he saved himself. He doesn't talk about the quality of his cry for help. He doesn't brag about how the man saved him because he was persistent (even though he was). All he can talk about is the man who saved him. He says nothing about his own part in that - for his part was nothing more than a feeble, but persistent cry for help. An important part, nonetheless, had he not cried out for help, He may have not been rescued at all and yet his focus is completely on his rescuer - as it should be!

Now I told you they were extremes and when you see the full implications of those extremes, they will be very confronting. You may not like them at all and may even struggle with my application, but please work with me here and allow God to use these extreme pictures to clarify this issue of pride when it comes to prayer.

I am not talking about our standing in Christ. You may already be racing ahead thinking, *"Hang on, I have already been rescued, once and for all; I am seated with Christ in the heavenlies; my position when I come to God in prayer is not that of one who is hanging over a cliff. I have already been rescued."* I totally agree, but I am talking about our attitude, our recognition of our relative place before God. I am talking about humility and pride. So, in light of that fact, let's get ready for what God is going to show us.

God is doing some truly wonderful stuff every day in so many people's lives in answer to prayer. I guess those two images, extreme as they are, serve as a powerful warning. We can so easily become like the Executive. It is so easy for us to lose our focus and take the glory away from God.

Anyone who knows me well will understand that I am a strong supporter of equipping and training and certainly, prayer is one of those areas in which we can be taught and trained - not with man-made techniques or formulas - but rather trained in our understanding of God and His heart and His grace and His generosity and our position before Him in prayer.

The more we know God; the more we abide in Him; the closer we get to Him; the greater our effectiveness in prayer. Why? Not because we learned how to negotiate stuff out of God like the Executive in our illustration; not because we have obtained skills of communication which give us a higher strike rate in the prayer department. The most important equipping we need is in the area of intimacy with God.

> *"Draw near to Me and I will draw near to you. Abide in me ... get to know me ... stick close to me ... know my heart and mind ... and you will get everything you ask for in accordance with My will."*

> *"Humble yourselves under the mighty hand of God and He will lift you up."* (Great verse for the man hanging over the cliff!)

> *"Blessed are the poor in spirit (those who know their poverty of spirit) for they will experience the power and majesty and glory of the Kingdom of God."*

That message is all the way through the Bible. Humility is the key to the door of the throne room of God - there is no other way in. As we get to know God more; as we draw closer to Him and He draws closer to us; we are even more humbled in His presence, but our trust and our faith grow - just as it does in human relationships. The more you know someone, the closer you get to them, the more you trust them and know their will and their character.

So, I guess I am saying that if you see the two pictures I gave you as two extreme ends of a continuum, then we need to be a lot closer in attitude to the guy hanging by a rope over a cliff than we are to the confident business Executive.

That does not minimise the importance of prayer and the benefit of the training and equipping which we may receive concerning prayer. God exhorts us to ask. He has given us this responsibility in our partnership with Him. I cannot allow any room for the fatalistic approach which says, *"God will do what God wants to do, regardless of what I do."*

That is inconsistent with most of what I am teaching in this very series and stands against many clear instructions in the Bible. Our responsibility in prayer is absolutely vital, yet our attitude in prayer is equally important because this insidious kind of pride will rob us of the beauty and the wonder of answered prayer and will rob God of the glory due His name.

When you want to report what God has done in answer to your prayer, you need to think very carefully about what your role really was in the whole prayer process. When God answers your prayer, stop at that point, and walk over to the mirror on the wall and look hard and long at the image you see. Do you see the self-confident Executive who just managed to get what he wanted from the Boss, or do you see the grateful and overwhelmed man who was just rescued by someone who cared enough to hear his feeble cry?

I don't care if you fasted and prayed for days; I don't care if you prayed in tongues and bound the enemy; I don't care if you have studied the principles of prayer and have tips and techniques coming out your ears! The bottom line is simple: you were on a rope hanging over a cliff, powerless to fix the problem yourself so you cried out for help (which is the beginning and end of your part in this) and someone else; someone other than you, chose to be in a place where they could hear you and they chose to heed your cry and help you. That should be your attitude, always and forever, when you come to God in prayer.

It doesn't matter who we are; what church we attend; what our attitude is to spiritual gifts; whether we shout or whisper; kneel or stand or dance; alone or in a group - we are all in exactly the same place of powerless dependency when we come to God in prayer and we all need to have the same attitude of humility.

In my mind's eye now, I can see a sweet, quiet, little old lady rugged up in front of the fire at home, praying day and night for her children and grandchildren and great grandchildren; day after day after month after year; she prays that they will find the Lord and be protected and safe.

I see the joy on her face when she finally learns that one of her little ones has been rescued by the Lord. No one will ever know what that lady prayed, she is seen by no one, heard by no one and has no one to report this miracle to, yet God is awesome and gracious and has heard the cry of His precious child.

By stark contrast, I can see a prominent preacher on a stage in front of 15,000 people in a healing crusade waving his hand and praying a prayer and watching hundreds of people fall under the power of the Spirit, healed in an instant from all manner of disease and deformity.

Everyone knows about that answer to prayer - the whole world can watch it on TV, and yet at the heart of that miracle, God is awesome and gracious and has simply heard the cry of His child. The setting, the volume, the exposure, the supposed 'anointing' on the preacher – that is all totally irrelevant.

Next time God answers your prayer, close your eyes and picture Him pulling you up on that rope over the cliff and then, only then, will you be able to report that to others in a way that exalts the Lord and not you. I believe there are many times when we should not even mention the fact that we prayed. I must be honest and say that I cringe, just a little, when people share answers to prayer and begin by telling us about what they did in order to get God to do something.

That may not be their intention, and I am not scolding anyone here, I am just delivering the warning which God needs us all to hear because this applies to us all. When God does something wonderful in answer to our prayers, why do we feel the need to share our part in that?

I know that it can sometimes build people's faith to hear that God does answer our prayers, but the Bible says we are to declare the wonderful works of God, day and night. It doesn't say we are to declare our fruitful prayers! Only a small difference in wording but there can be a huge difference in attitude.

When God answers your prayers and you feel you want to glorify Him for that, then go ahead and do just that - glorify <u>God</u>. Shout it from the mountain top if you like: *"Our God is so awesome ... let me tell you what He has done this week ... let me declare His wonderful works."* Sometimes it will be relevant for people to know that you prayed, but most of the time, that will only serve to put you in the spotlight instead of God.

Now don't misunderstand me here. There is no great crime in telling people you prayed - even David in the Psalms did it when he said often, *"I sought the Lord, and he heard me..."* It is the attitude of our heart that matters. We just need to understand that those listening to us may not know our heart and we may inadvertently draw some of the glory from God in the way we report what God has done.

Let us be very careful then, lest we rob God of His glory and give people the wrong impression of what prayer is all about. I know I am on thin ice with many people in the Body of Christ in even addressing this issue, and yet it is so very important, and I see pride creeping in so often. If humility does not saturate our being before, during and after coming to God in prayer, we are setting ourselves up for a really rough ride.

Let me cut right to the bone here - when we adopt the prideful, man-centred Business Executive position in prayer, even if only in part; if we think that the quality of our presentation, the words we use, the technique we adopt, the time we spend, the language we adopt - anything at all to do with us - is what secures the answer to our prayer, then not only are we proud, arrogant and deceived at that point, we are setting ourselves and those around us up for a huge fall.

Before we brag (unintentionally, maybe) about a prayer we prayed which God answered, we need to ask ourselves why we prayed in the first place. Was it our compassion, our insight, our concern for someone which prompted our prayer? Perhaps. Or was it the Holy Spirit laying a burden on our heart to pray for that person or situation?

I believe the Bible when it tells me that my fallen human heart in its natural state is wicked, selfish, and oblivious to anyone but me! So, if I find myself in prayer, crying out to God to intervene in some situation in my life or the Church or others I care about, I have no doubt whatsoever that the Spirit of God led me to that point – nothing in me would do that. So, God gets the glory at the beginning and the end of the whole process of prayer – as it should be.

Assuming you are still reading, allow me to probe a little deeper. What we do when the answers to our prayers are not what we expect or want, will be determined by our attitude to God and ourselves before and during that prayer.

When you give it your best shot before God and the outcome is the opposite of what you prayed - where do you go with that? What do you do with that?

I know where many people go, they go to a place Satan prepares for those whose attitude to God and prayer is completely wrong and they begin to doubt themselves and ultimately, they might even doubt God.

> *"If only I had prayed longer, harder, more often, in the Spirit; I should have fasted; I should have called others to pray with me; if only I had repented of that habitual sin that I still struggle with; if only I had done this or that ..."*

What torture we endure when we set ourselves higher than God in prayer! I know people who 'pray the blood of the lamb' over their house and family every day; others who 'put on the armour of God in prayer' every morning. When they forget to do that, and something invariably goes wrong that day - they attribute it to something they did or didn't do.

These are tools of the flesh dressed up to look spiritual. When prayers like this are prayed in some ritualistic, even magical manner, they are closer to witchcraft than any of us would want to think.

They are nothing but spiritual formulas designed to move the hand of God or worse still, spiritual 'spells' we cast each day. That is not prayer! God wants a relationship - not works of the flesh - that is why He calls us to humble ourselves, pray, seek His face and remove all barriers to that intimacy. Then, His hand will move.

But even then, He is still God, and we are not, and stuff will happen which we do not like or understand. People get sick; accidents happen; tragedy strikes, and people die - even when so many in the body of Christ are praying otherwise. When that happens, our God should receive no less glory than when we get what we ask for.

We can cry out to God and ask Him anything we like, and He will always listen - but there will be times when we don't get the result we want and our response to God at that moment will reveal much about our relationship with Him, our faith in Him and our trust of Him.

When tragedy strikes; when things don't go well; when our prayers seem to have no effect; we have a choice: we can rob God of His glory and walk around in a daze, scratching our heads and wondering what when wrong. Sooner or later that kind of thinking causes us to withdraw from God so far that we stop asking for anything.

Alternatively, we can determine that God will be glorified in everything, and we can fall to our knees and say with Job after he had just lost everything in his life that mattered other than God:

> "Naked I came from my mother's womb ... naked I shall return ... blessed be the name of the Lord."

And we can join Jesus in the Garden of anguish and tears the night His Father said no to his request to take the cup from Him ... as He gave glory to God and said:

> "Not my will, but yours be done O Lord."

And we can join with the apostle Paul when he penned these powerful words …

> *"Oh, the depth of the riches of the wisdom and knowledge of God! How unsearchable his judgments, and his paths beyond tracing out! "Who has known the mind of the Lord? Or who has been his counsellor?"*

> *"Who has ever given to God, that God should repay them?" For from him and through him and for him are all things. To him be the glory forever! Amen." (Romans 11:33-36)*

6. Pride exalts in being made much of

This area is closely linked to the last one, but I believe it deserves special mention as it has some unique characteristics. I find it fascinating to look at the life and ministry of Jesus and examine what He spent His time doing and saying in those few short years of ministry. Who did He share His precious time with and what were the themes of His teaching?

When I look at the amount of time, effort and money spent today by some church leaders as they embark upon moral crusades against abortion, homosexuality, gambling, and other social problems, I confess I am puzzled to know where they got that agenda from. Such crusades are not seen in the ministry of Jesus.

All those problems were present in the society back then, plus some and yet we do not see Jesus on His soapbox preaching against such things.

What we do see, however, is that the few times Jesus did get hot under the collar and speak very strongly against the sins of His day, it was usually addressed to the senior Pastors and religious leaders of the day (the Pharisees) and the subject, more often than not, was pride.

In Matthew 23 we have some of the strongest words our Lord ever spoke when Jesus really laid it on the line powerfully with the religious leaders. Read the whole chapter some time! It is actually quite shocking!

"And they love the place of honour at banquets, and the chief seats in the synagogues, and respectful greetings in the marketplaces, and being called by men, Rabbi." (Matthew 23:6)

One of the ugliest, but most common manifestations of pride can be seen in people who exalt themselves above their position. This is particularly applicable to people in leadership or people who aspire to be in leadership.

Having an 'up-front' role in any ministry carries this risk of self-exaltation. The danger is there all the time that people see you and not Jesus. They can see your personal gifts, rather than His gifts, given to the church, through you. Some of this may be unavoidable and has more to do with other people's views of you. However, much of the danger emerges from the attitude of the person in leadership.

Let me comment first about those in leadership positions already - the ones who currently have up-front roles in the church. Perhaps you lead a ministry or a small group; perhaps you are a Deacon or Elder or worship leader; or you may teach or preach. Regardless of the actual role, you are a prime target for the enemy in this area of self-exaltation and unless you are alert to the dangers, you will find yourself falling into his trap.

Those in leadership must never forget that leadership in the Body of Christ is always servant-leadership. It is functional leadership. It is Christ-like leadership. As servant-leaders, we are called to always serve the needs of others above our own and we need to have their well-being upper-most in our minds.

Functional leadership means we are appointed and called to do a job, achieve an outcome, fulfil a ministry. We are not appointed to hold an office or elevate our status. Our 'title' is merely a designation of our specific responsibility – nothing more. Christ-like leadership, as the name suggests, means that ultimately, we follow the example of Jesus – which means we lay our whole life on the line for those we lead. If we always keep these things in mind, they will be a safeguard against pride of self-exaltation.

There are many gifted people in leadership in the church and the risk is always present that they will begin to think they 'possess' certain gifts and abilities and are in some way responsible for them.

There's no doubt that we have a role in the development of the gifts we are given, but we must never forget that God gives gifts to the church - not to individuals.

In Romans 12:6, Paul tells us that we all have different gifts according to the grace given to us by God. These are not gifts which we pick and choose – and he reminds us that even the level of faith and grace we enjoy is measured out by God. Paul makes this even clearer in his letter to the Ephesians:

> *"But to each one of us grace has been given as Christ apportioned it … It was he who gave some to be apostles, some to be prophets, some to be evangelists, and some to be pastors and teachers, to prepare God's people for works of service, so that the body of Christ may be built up until we all reach unity in the faith and in the knowledge of the Son of God and become mature, attaining to the whole measure of the fullness of Christ." (Ephesians 4:7,11-13)*

Our measure of grace and the gifts we have are determined by the Head of the Church, the Lord Jesus Christ and the desired effect of that grace and the purpose of those gifts is not to exalt us. The purpose is to bless the church and build up the body of Christ.

Those of us in leadership positions need to always keep these truths in the front of our minds and be alert to the enemy's schemes in trying to push us into the spotlight all the time and rob God of the glory that is due to Him alone.

Now there is a much wider implication to this manifestation of pride than just current leaders. This warning applies to all of us and particularly to those who struggle with their role in the church and may be seeking a more up-front ministry.

This is a good springboard for me to talk about a very common problem I see in the Body of Christ – one in which pride can play a major role. There is this cancerous lie which eats away at the heart of the church which tries to convince people that the important ministries are the visible ministries. If we can be seen in our service of God, then it is a more important position. That is why up-front positions and leadership roles are more highly coveted and sought-after than the less visible roles.

This lie can have some disastrous effects in the church. The most common thing that happens when people believe this lie is that those whom God has gifted in such vital areas as service, pastoral care, prayer, and other foundational ministries, become restless because they are not being noticed or appreciated as much as those who are more visible. If this restlessness is not identified and dealt with early, it leads these people out of their area of gifting in search of more visible ministries. They neglect the gifts God has given them and start pursuing other areas of ministry which seem more important, regardless of their gifting.

The reason this happens so often is that these people are not aware of most of what is happening. They are not intentionally being prideful or arrogant. They are deceived and they have allowed the enemy to down-play the vital importance of their gifts and ministry and lead them to seek fulfilment in an area to which God has not called them. God's bidding is God's enabling and He will never call someone into a ministry without giving them the necessary gifts and skills. Yet there are thousands of people all over the world who are Pastors, Elders, Deacons, and ministry leaders who should never have taken on such a role. They are operating outside their calling … and beyond their 'spiritual turf.'

They are well-meaning and probably genuine in their desire to serve God, but they are not being true to the gifts God has given the church through them. Their motivation for moving into a more up-front ministry is not correct and so the Church is robbed of their true gifting until they recognise it and operate within the boundaries God has set for them at the point in time.

Then there are the people who deep down really do know their gifts and their calling and yet they are not satisfied to stay within the boundaries of that gifting. They are the people who are not faithful with the small things and patient in waiting for God to reveal more. They run ahead of God in their impatience and unbridled enthusiasm and make deliberate choices to take on tasks and ministries which are beyond them because they are not satisfied with their current lot.

Such people will often aspire to leadership roles for which they are not gifted and to which God has not called them. Such people may find themselves involved in overseas mission work without first being tested and proven faithful in a local mission context. This is being addressed more and more by a number of mission organisations, but it is still a problem.

Too many sincere believers end up serving in short-term and long-term overseas mission work who have not had those gifts or that calling really tested and proven in a local ministry context. Many of these people may have a genuine passion for overseas mission, but many more are attracted to the importance of such work in contrast to the less glamorous hard work on the local scene.

Yet the Bible reminds us of the importance of being faithful in the small things and proving faithful with what we have already been given before we seek after something more. Perhaps the most powerful passage Jesus gave us is the parable of the talents which is summed up in the concluding verse:

> *"Well done! Good and faithful servant. You have been faithful with a few things; I will put you in charge of many things."*
> (*Matthew 25:21*)

There are many believers who are not faithful with a few things … they actually ignore them and even despise the lesser things in favour of those things which they regard as more important, more interesting, or more noticeable. Paul warns us strongly to not make such judgments about that which God ordains.

"But in fact, God has arranged the parts in the body, every one of them, just as he wanted them to be. If they were all one part, where would the body be? As it is, there are many parts, but one body. The eye cannot say to the hand, "I don't need you!"

And the head cannot say to the feet, "I don't need you!" On the contrary, those parts of the body that seem to be weaker are indispensable, and the parts that we think are less honourable we treat with special honour. And the parts that are unpresentable are treated with special modesty, while our presentable parts need no special treatment.

But God has combined the members of the body and has given greater honour to the parts that lacked it, so that there should be no division in the body, but that its parts should have equal concern for each other. If one part suffers, every part suffers with it; if one part is honoured, every part rejoices with it. Now you are the body of Christ, and each one of you is a part of it."
(1 Corinthians 12:18-27)

God arranges the parts of the body. God distributes the gifts and skills. God calls people into their various ministries and determines where they should bear the most fruit. That is why we must identify and affirm the gifts of God in each other and encourage people in that gifting and discourage and stop people from operating outside their gifting - for that is not what God has apportioned to them and God will not be exalted unless they submit to His plan and purpose for them at every stage in their lives.

There are countless well-meaning believers who have been severely beaten up by the enemy and have inflicted major damage in the Church because they fail to understand this basic, but vital truth. Please make sure you are not one of them!

7. Pride aspires to the place of God

The story of Herod is one of many we could quote here:

"And on an appointed day Herod, having put on his royal apparel, took his seat on the rostrum, and began delivering an address to them. And the people kept crying out, "The voice of a god and not of a man!"

And immediately an angel of the Lord struck him because he did not give God the glory, and he was eaten by worms and died." *(Acts 12:21-23)*

This one act did not bring the wrath of God on its own - but a whole life devoted to playing God resulted in Herod's demise. Pride can have disastrous effects if not exposed.

8. Pride opposes the very existence of God

"In his pride the wicked man does not seek him; in all his thoughts there is no room for God." *(Psalm 10:4)*

Pride knows that by far the simplest solution for its own survival would be that there is no God at all. That would be, as the Nazi's might say, "*The Final Solution*" for the survival of pride. It doesn't come as any surprise then that:

9. Pride refuses to trust in God

Pride cannot trust God. The posture of trust is just too weak and too dependent. Trust calls too much attention to the strength and wisdom of another. But trusting God is the heartbeat of humility. Trusting God is the absolute opposite of pride.

When pride keeps us from trusting God to take care of us, there are two possibilities: one is that we feel a false security based on our own imagined power and ability, and the other is that we realize that we cannot guarantee our security, and so we feel anxious and fearful. Either way – pride is at work.

I believe that a lack of trust in God lies at the heart of so many of our woes today. The Bible is full of the promises of God to His people and every one of those promises can be a reality to those who trust God to be true to His word.

God has promised to care for us and protect us and yet we are anxious and fearful, and we go to incredible lengths to pray special prayers of protection or create weird kinds of spiritual formulae in order to 'feel' like we are protected. That is pride. That is human effort to achieve something only God can do. God said He will protect His children. We either accept that and trust Him to be true to His promise … or we don't.

As believers, we can sometimes find ourselves in some financial difficulties. Again, God has asked us to trust Him in this area too. He wants us to be wise and frugal and sensible in managing our money … but He wants us to trust Him to guide us in that process.

Let's not expect God to undo our bad financial decisions – He can't do that - but trusting Him to help us make better choices and then believing He will supply all real our needs, is another sign of submission and humility.

The bottom line for most of us comes down to a simple question: *"How big is our God?"* When we look at how much we worry and fret about some things, we must confess that our level of trust makes God pretty small. We need to study the promises of God more and stand on those promises more and allow the Spirit of God to release trust in us.

That process of relying on someone else to care for us and protect us and provide for our needs will, in itself, release humility in us before God and those around us. Truly humble people have a high level of trust in God – the two go hand-in-hand. This all leads to our final manifestation of pride which I covered in some detail in a previous chapter – so I will just touch on it again here.

10. Pride is anxious about the future

God says to anxious Israel that their problem is pride:

> " … *even I, am He who comforts you. Who are you that you are afraid of man who dies, and of the son of man who is made like grass; that you have forgotten the Lord your Maker?"*
> *(Isaiah 51:12-13)*

What a confronting word from God for today! *Who do you think you - being afraid!?* Sounds a little strange don't you think? But that's how subtle pride is. Pride is the root of our anxiety. Now we can see clearly and feel the force of Peter's words here:

> *"Humble yourselves, therefore, under God's mighty hand, that he may lift you up in due time ..."* How? In what way shall you humble yourselves? *Answer (v. 7): by, "casting all your anxiety upon Him, because He cares for you." (1 Peter 5:6-7)*

In other words, the most humble thing in the world we can do is trust God with everything in every way. Casting your anxieties on God means trusting the promise that He really does care for you and has the power and the wisdom to put that care to work in the most glorious way.

As has already been stated, that kind of trust is the opposite of pride and the essence of humility. It's the confidence that the mighty hand of God is not over you to crush you, but to care for you just like the promise says.

I have spent a lot of time on this issue of humility and pride and rightly so. For as I have stated many times now, we cannot proceed in our study of 2 Chronicles 7:14 with any degree of confidence unless we understand the foundational necessity of humility in the whole process of seeking the face of God and believing for Him to heal our land.

It is in our weakness that His strength will be revealed; it is our broken, contrite, humble posture before God every day which is the key to His heavenly Throne-room and the secret to the abundant fruitful life He has planned for each of us.

CHAPTER ELEVEN

Prayer: The Heart of the Matter

We come now to one of the most important words in this entire verse. In fact, when our study of this verse is over, we may conclude that this one word is the essence of this verse and that everything written before and after this word points to it and follow from it. Of course, that word is PRAY.

> *"If my people who are called by my name will humble themselves and **pray** ..." (2 Chronicles 7:14a)*

Prayer lies at the heart of this exhortation. God is asking those who are called by His name, to prepare themselves to pray, and He promises that He will hear their prayers and heal their land. Prayer is so central and so vital in this verse and in our whole experience of God, that I will taking two chapters to explore the nature, purpose, and priority of prayer.

This verse does not say that the God will heal the land if His people humble themselves. Humility is the position we must take in order to pray and seek the face of God. Prayer lies at the heart of it all and it especially lies at the heart of revival.

I believe all sincere Christians desire a dynamic and fruitful prayer life. Yet so many find themselves defeated when it comes to their communication with God. If the average church member were to be asked how much time he or she spends in prayer, many would be too embarrassed to answer the question. That's not a criticism - just a statement of fact. Yet, prayer holds the key to developing intimacy with God and consistency in our walk with Him.

There is a significant difference between religious praying and Christian praying. Most praying today consists of religious duty rather than genuine Christian praying. Muslims pray. Jews pray. Hindus pray. So, what's the difference in Christian praying and religious praying?

Religious praying is man's attempt to reach up to God. However, genuine Christian praying is God making a way for us to enter into His presence and have fellowship with Him.

God is holy and so it would be impossible for anyone or anything unholy to come into His presence. That's the whole reason that Jesus died on the cross 2,000 years ago. When Jesus died, the Bible says, "*At that moment the curtain of the temple was torn in two from top to bottom.*" (Matthew 27:51). The curtain was that which separated the holy of holies, from the holy place.

Under the old covenant, only the high priest was allowed to enter the holy of holies because that was considered the place where one would encounter the manifest presence of God. A sinful man or woman could not enter into the presence of a Holy God. But when Jesus died, He brought forgiveness for our sin and provided cleansing for all who embraced His gift of salvation. Therefore, by the grace of God, we have access into the presence of Almighty God.

Think about that. You and I, by the blood that Jesus shed on the cross, can now enter into the very presence of the Creator of the universe. That's Christian praying. Coming to God - not by our own religious works of righteousness - but by His grace.

That changes the whole concept of prayer. It's no longer duty, it's delight. It's not religion, but relationship. It's not defeat, it's victory - victorious Christian praying.

To become victorious in our prayer lives, we must understand the true nature of prayer. The first step in victorious Christian praying is an understanding that prayer is God's invitation, by His grace, for each of us to enter into His presence.

The Bible describes the throne of God as the "*throne of grace.*" (Hebrews 4:16). The only way that we can approach an absolutely holy God is by His grace. When we understand that great truth, then prayer becomes dynamic, and peace and joy flow from our time with God.

Every morning, we should stand amazed in the presence of God. When we come into His presence, it's not to get something from Him, although He gives us more than we could ever ask or think of asking. We don't try to twist His arm. Rather, we try to bend our heart to merge with His heart.

The primary purpose in coming into the presence of God is to get to know Him personally, intimately and deeply. It's experiencing Him fully. Prayer is the practical method of developing a love-relationship with God the Father, Son and Holy Spirit. There's nothing boring or ritualistic about that! It is an unparalleled adventure! Getting to know the One Who knows everyone and everything! What a privilege! What an awesome blessing!

Prayer is the communion of two hearts - the heart of God and the heart of His children. God's heart is absolutely pure and holy. His heart is the almighty, eternal heart. Our hearts are the tiny, impure, deceitful-above-all-things hearts. Yet, by the blood of Jesus, we are granted entrance into His presence. Wow! That's victorious praying. Just getting to know God - by His grace.

Now in the context of 2 Chronicles 7:14, we see this vital link between prayer and revival. God has promised that if His people humble themselves and **pray** … He will heal their land. We all want revival … we all want to see our land healed by God … but we don't all want to pray like we should and like we must if we want to see that revival come.

Over 160 years ago, the great English Baptist pastor, Charles Haddon Spurgeon, wrote the following:

> "*The times of refreshing from the presence of the Lord have at last dawned upon our land. Everywhere there are signs of aroused activity and increased earnestness. A spirit of prayer is visiting our churches … The first breath of the rushing mighty wind is already discerned, while on the rising of evangelists the tongue of fire has evidently descended.*"

The "spirit of prayer" that Spurgeon described has always been at the root of every great awakening of the Christian Church. It matters not whether you search the New Testament or look in the halls of history, revival has always been preceded by prayer. In Acts 1, the Church was birthed in a prayer meeting. In the next chapter, we read where 3,000 people were converted to Christ. Throughout the book of the Acts, when the Church prayed, God responded, in so many incredible ways!

The first great missions' movement was birthed in prayer. Time and time again, the Church took great strides forward because someone or a small band of people prayed. Victorious praying lays the foundation for revival.

Over the last several decades, I've studied many of the great evangelical revivals in history, and I've discovered a simple truth: all revivals have prayer at the heart of them. Someone gets a burden and begins to pray. They wait upon the Lord and in His divine time, He answers their prayers. They meet with God and God minister to them and then through them.

I would not try and make you believe that I understand all the reasons why that is so. I just know it's a spiritual law of life. It's true. Prayer and revival are always partners in the manifestation of the glory of God. His glory comes when He comes. When that happens, the Church is accelerated in its spiritual and numerical growth. Revival precedes great harvests of souls, and prayer always precedes great revivals in the church.

In its simplest form, prayer is intimacy with God. When we become intimate with Him, then we're on the road to revival. We can't be intimate with God and wear a religious mask. Genuine prayer produces genuine repentance. Deep repentance releases the Spirit of God in our lives. When that happens, then we are already on the road to revival. The church was born in a prayer meeting, and it was sustained by God through men and women of prayer. While fervent prayer seems to be the abnormal experience of believers today, it was the norm in first-century Christianity.

In Acts chapter one, we find the Church crying out to God. In the next chapter, Peter and John are going to a prayer meeting when God heals a lame man. In Acts chapter four, the Church is seeking God's face. All through the book of Acts, the Church is found in a position of absolute dependence upon God. The church not only prayed during those early days of its history, but it also grew - so rapidly that the Scriptures record that thousands were added daily to the church. Historians tell us that the church had a phenomenal growth rate for many, many years.

It's interesting to note that prayer has always been a propelling force in the church. The great historic revivals have always had their silent heroes of prayer. It's the one indisputable common denominator of the revived church. A fresh passion to reach the world is birthed in the revived church. The pattern normally goes something like this. The church slips into lethargy; that always leads to moral impurity and spiritual apathy; the church may be asleep, but the Holy Spirit isn't. The Spirit begins to stir in the hearts of a faithful remnant, and they begin crying out to God for revival and renewal. God responds to their cries and begins to arouse the passions of the prophets and teachers. They begin proclaiming God's word with renewed power and the sleeping giant begins to wake up. Sins are confessed. Repentance grips the hearts of God's people, and a passion for the lost starts to overwhelm those who have experienced Christ's forgiveness. The result is that multitudes are born into the kingdom of God.

This pattern has been an historic reality, repeated over and over again. Prayer is always a precursor of great spiritual revivals. It's the expression of humble hearts. Genuine prayer says, *"God, we need you. Without You, we can do nothing."* Absolute dependence upon God is a prerequisite to a mighty move of God.

Revival is the manifest grace of God upon His people. That grace is always released in and through humble hearts. *"God opposes the proud but gives grace to the humble."* (James 4:6). God hates pride as we well know from this teaching, but He's tender and merciful towards the humble. The humble, praying church always sets the stage for the revived church.

Prayer has not only preceded revivals throughout Biblical times, but it's been at the inception of every great historical revival of the church. God's hand was mightily upon John Wesley and George Whitefield during the eighteenth century. God used them both to bring multitudes into the kingdom of God. George Whitefield was especially used by God to spark revival in the early history of the United States. Arnold Dallimore, biographer of Whitefield, wrote of what took place, in Whitefield's words:

"Early in the morning, at noonday, evening and midnight, nay, all day long, did the blessed Jesus visit and refresh my heart. Could the trees of a certain wood near Stonehouse speak, they would tell what sweet communion I and some others enjoyed with the ever-blessed God there ... I would be so overpowered with God's Infinite Majesty that I would be constrained to throw myself on the ground and offer my soul as a blank in His hands, to write on it what He pleased."

What was the result of such praying? Whitefield described it beautifully:

"I preached about five times a week, but the congregations grew larger and larger. It was wonderful to see how the people hung upon the rails of the organ loft, climbed upon the leads of the church, and made the church so hot with their breath that the steam would fall from the pillars like drops of rain. Sometimes almost as many would go away for want of room as came in."

The secret to the great revival of the 1700s was that God found men and women of prayer. God has not changed. What He did then, He is more than willing to do today. The only question is whether we have changed since those revival days.

We live in a time when we tend to think that it's by our human talent and ingenuity that we'll reach the world, rather than by God's power. However, the fact is, the growing churches around the world who are bringing new people into the Kingdom every day are the praying Churches. God is still on His throne. He has not changed. He revives His people when they pray and seek His face. It has been true historically, and it's still true today.

The promise of 2 Chronicles 7:14 is a promise about prayer. This whole verse is about prayer and revival and the promise of God that the two will go hand in hand. God hasn't changed. He will revive His people today just as He's done throughout history. He will do so, as we pray.

There has been a pattern in the great soul harvests throughout the history of the church. It was the pattern of the dynamic fast-growing church in Jerusalem as recorded in the Acts of the Apostles. The Bible says, *"After they prayed, the place where they were meeting was shaken. And they were all filled with the Holy Spirit and spoke the word of God boldly."* (Acts 4:31).

There were four things that took place according to the Scripture. First, they prayed. Second, God shook everything up. Third, they were all filled with the Holy Spirit. Finally, they had a new power to speak the word of God with courage.

The end result of prayer was evangelism. When we draw near to God, we are filled with His presence. He is love, and His perfect love casts out all fear. That's why they had power to speak with boldness. They had been in the presence of the One who is absolute love. Fear flees in the presence of Divine love. A praying church will always become an evangelistic church. Evangelism and revival aren't the same things, but when we pray, we're already on the road to revival, and when revival genuinely takes hold, evangelism is the supernatural natural result.

Evangelism is on the heart of God. The Bible clearly tells us that God loves His lost and dying world. The whole mission of Jesus was summed up in His words, *"I came to seek and to save the lost."* The world is always on the heart of God, and the world ought to be on the hearts of God's people. When it is, then we'll begin to weep for those who've never come to know the Saviour.

Prayer is the secret to evangelistic outreach. Prayer is intimacy with God and when we are intimate with God, we'll seek His kingdom to come in the hearts and lives of the people around us.

Humble, holy, praying men and women have always been God's weapons in evangelism. He is still searching for such people because prayer always prepares the heart of an unbelieving generation. Jesus said, "*No one can come to me unless the Father has enabled him.*" (John 6:65).

We don't reach people with the message of Christ because we're super salespeople or great orators. We get through to people because God the Holy Spirit has done a deep work in their hearts. It's because the Spirit has drawn them to Jesus. Prayer releases the Holy Spirit to those who are yet to taste delights in God's kingdom. God's method hasn't changed. He's still looking for humble, holy praying men, women, and young people. When He finds such people, watch out! All the resources of heaven will be released, and the spiritually blind will see and broken hearts will be mended.

Let me tell you a story finish this first chapter on prayer. It was an historic moment. Thousands had gathered in the stadium in Moldova for the first time ever to hear the gospel of Jesus Christ. At that time, Moldova was still a part of the former Soviet Union. Christians were persecuted. Life was difficult. Everyone had been brainwashed with atheism. But Christians had prayed for God to open the doors, and this was that day.

The preacher, an evangelist from Texas, was very nervous as he stood to proclaim the name of Christ. Questions filled his mind. What would the people think? Would they respond to an open invitation to come to Christ? Several years earlier he had been deported from the Soviet Union for telling university students about Jesus. Now, he stood at this historic moment to proclaim the great gift of God's salvation.

At the close of his message that afternoon, he extended the invitation for people to come to Christ. At first, he asked people to lift their hands if they wanted to know Christ, and he told them that he would pray for them. No one lifted a hand. He prayed, "*Oh God, what do I do now?*" The Holy Spirit seemed to whisper in his heart, "*Press on. Press on.*"

He then called for people to join him at the front of the platform if they wanted to place their faith in Christ and follow Him. No one responded. He prayed again, but God seemed to indicate that He had everything all under control. He looked up, and to his surprise, a poor peasant woman came out of the stands all by herself. She was carrying a bouquet of flowers over her head. She marched all by herself in front of an overflow crowd in the stadium, right up to the pulpit. She then handed the preacher the flowers and knelt in front of the pulpit and began to cry out to God in deep travail. Her prayers echoed through the stadium.

As she began to pray, the Holy Spirit swept through the stadium with awesome power. Tens, then twenties, then fifties, and then hundreds of people began to respond to the invitation to come to Christ. It was an incredible sight to behold. Close to 2,500 people committed their lives to Jesus Christ that afternoon. The preacher was so moved by the courage of that one poor peasant woman that he wrote the story of what had happened in his newsletter. He actually had pictures of what took place.

Not long after the newsletter was sent out, he received a phone call from a lady who had been in a women's prayer group with the preacher's wife. She said, "*Can I come to your office? There's something that I must show you.*" She came to him and brought her prayer diary with her. Every day she would record how God had impressed upon her the need to pray. She had been praying for two months for that Moldovan crusade.

God had laid it on her heart to pray specifically for one poor peasant woman in Moldova "*to have the courage to do whatever God was telling her to do.*" She had recorded those exact words in her diary consistently as she prayed, not knowing what they meant or what God had planned.

One woman in San Antonio, Texas prayed, and God shook an entire nation. Prayer prepared the heart of one peasant woman, and God was able to work a miracle. I believe that when we get to heaven, we'll discover that the true heroes of our faith aren't necessarily the great platform personalities.

They won't necessarily be those well known to the world, but they will certainly be those well known to God - those who have tarried in the quiet place of prayer.

> *(Jesus said), "But when you pray, go into your room, close the door and pray to your Father, who is unseen. Then your Father, who sees what is done in secret, will reward you."(Matthew 6:6)*

One day we will all discover who God's secret heroes have been. They are those who wrote the history of the kingdom with the secret prayers of their hearts. I would not try to make you believe that I understand all the reasons why that is so. I just know it's true. Prayer and revival are always partners in the manifestation of the glory of God. His glory comes when God comes. When that happens, the church is accelerated in its spiritual and in its numerical growth. Revival precedes great harvests of souls, and prayer always precedes great revivals of the church.

CHAPTER TWELVE

Prayer: The Means to a Greater End

I want to say something that may sound contradictory, but bear with me and you will soon understand what I mean. As I said in an earlier chapter, like *humility*, I believe the *prayer* is a vital key in 2 Chronicles 7:14, and indeed our whole Christian life. However, this verse is not really about prayer. When understood correctly, prayer is the means by which we develop something far greater: *relationship*.

I am not playing word games here. Prayer is the vehicle which takes us somewhere. Prayer is the means by which we develop something else. It doesn't take a high IQ to work that out from reading the Bible. Prayer is not an end in itself - it is a means to a far greater end.

Sadly, there are millions of Christians all over the world who have been subtly coerced into making prayer an end goal. Prayer becomes the destination. Thousands of books have been written about prayer - teaching us how to have a good prayer life as though a 'prayer life' is the goal. Prayer is the means by which we have intimate communion with God. Therefore, prayer is a means to a far greater end: *a meaningful, fruitful relationship with God*. This is so simple that I am almost embarrassed to point it out, but I fear that it's a simple truth that has somehow been lost in the middle of a whole mass of teaching about prayer.

We need to realise just how subtle the enemy of God is and how easy it is for him to twist things God has given us in a way that turns them into religion and surely by now we are aware that Satan will replace relationship with religion at every possible point. We don't have to open that door very far before the enemy is through it in a flash.

Prayer is one of those precious, beautiful, personal, powerful gifts which God has bestowed upon His children. Have you ever thought about the privilege of prayer?

How incredible is this gift? The God Who created this universe and keeps the earth spinning on its axis; the God Who holds all of creation together and keeps you breathing - actually invites you to come into His presence, relax and chat about life and the universe and anything else you want to talk about. Prayer is a wonderful gift - it is not a method to be used to get something from God. Sadly, however, in so many ways over the years, we have allowed Satan to turn prayer into a dry, cold, calculating religious work or worse still, the currency with which we 'buy' things from God that we need.

Some of us may have come out of traditional, religious church backgrounds where prayers were prayed in Latin or such old-style English no one could relate to them anyway. Some of us grew up thinking that prayers were the things printed in a green book you read from each Sunday or someone up front did, and you just said amen. Don't get me wrong – God can still move through liturgy and formal prayers – but only if people have the ability to connect to the heart of those prayers. Then it is their hearts God moves through – not the prayers.

At some point we left that world and came to a church where people talk to God personally and intimately and prayer took on whole new meaning and power. Praise God for such a revelation. However, the danger remains high, for there is a new kind of religion emerging. This brand of religion is far more powerful and far more pervasive and destructive and far harder to fight than anything in the past. It is not the religion of the dead, cold, orthodox Church. It is a religion that has sprung up in the middle of the most dynamic, active, alive and 'successful' sections of the church. That is why it is so hard to fight.

It is difficult to stand in the midst of a crowd of happy, fulfilled, excited, productive, positive people and issue a warning about religion. That is why Satan is having such a great time, because very few people are brave enough (or suicidal enough) to stand up and say anything, and the few that do, may have personal axes to grind which cause them to become critical and they attack personalities rather than issues and false teaching.

I don't want to attack anyone, much less a fellow believer who is preaching what they think to be the Word of Truth. However, I do need to ring some alarm bells here because some of the most influential teachers in the church today, some of whom you will see on television if you wake up early enough, are marketing a 'gospel' which is contrary to what is clearly taught in the New Testament and that particularly applies to the issue of prayer, which is our primary focus in this chapter.

Every day, right across the world, millions of people are told that prayer has power. Actually, they are told that the 'right kind of prayer' has power. In fact, as I researched prayer for this book, I encountered people over and over again who spoke of the power of prayer and gave all the tips and principles and techniques so that we can be sure we are using the right words and praying the right way. I have whole books that deal with the issue of prayer - books by world-renown authors - and they are full of teaching which portrays prayer as this highly technical and complicated activity that only the spiritually elite can do well. What utter nonsense. In fact, it is demonic!

Prayer does not protect us - <u>God</u> protects us. Prayer does not heal us - <u>God</u> heals us. Prayer is not an exact science which we need to learn to do a certain way for it to work well. Saturating yourself with Scriptures about healing in order to build your faith before you pray to God to heal someone, sounds harmless enough. But just analyse what is happening there. Who are you trying to convince, yourself or God? When I hear some people pray, I am sure they are trying to convince God that He wants to heal, can heal and will heal. Prayer is communication and like all communication we can certainly get better at it – but when we are talking about communicating with God, we need to be so careful we don't slip into the trap of thinking that it was our prayer that healed someone or not.

I have a powerful memory of a ministry time in a conference in Sydney when Dr. Ken Blue was here back in 1993. My wife and I were in the middle of a three-week intensive Pastors school, and this was a weekend conference we helping to run.

At the end of a teaching session, one of the Pastors with us at the conference was being prayed for. He had suffered a chronic lung condition for many years. Ken and a few others gathered around this brother to pray. A few people prayed and then Ken prayed. It was a passionate prayer, a confident prayer. Ken obviously knew that God could heal, and he was believing that for this brother at that moment. He didn't need more faith or the right words - he had seen God heal thousands of times in situations like this - and he had seen Him not heal too.

At the end of the prayer, it was clear that nothing had happened right there and then. So, Ken said *"Amen"* ... pushed his chair back and stood up and said, *"Well, that's my best prayer. Bless you brother. Maybe next time."* With that he slapped his brother on the back and left. I remember thinking how pastorally insensitive, even arrogant that was to say to someone who had just <u>not</u> been healed.

However, I came to realise that it was the most honest and God-honouring thing I have ever heard someone say. In his own abrupt manner, Ken was reminding us, *"If God isn't doing it tonight, then He isn't doing it. No amount of naming, claiming, ranting or raving is going to change that. Our job is to pray, believing. God's job is to heal whenever He chooses to heal."*

Would Ken pray again for this man, if asked? Absolutely, and he did, the day before he left Australia - standing outside a public toilet block in fact. No conference; no music in the background; no faith-building sermon; no witnesses; just a simple prayer - and guess what? God healed this brother on the spot - right there and then, of a condition that he had suffered for 15 years!

I will never forget that night when Ken said, *"Well, that's my best prayer!"* Whenever I start down the road of thinking that the quality of my prayer or the words I use or the methods I employ is what moves the hand of God, the Holy Spirit reminds me of that night, and I laugh and realise how arrogant and proud we can become sometimes. I only wish every disciple of Jesus would understand this same truth.

That is not the case I am afraid, for there is a whole school of teaching now, under the banner of the 'word of faith' movement which stretches the bounds of the New Testament even further and tells us how vitally important the actual spoken word is and that we need to learn all this stuff before we can pray powerfully and effectively because we might be using the wrong words.

We also have people telling us how important it is to 'pray the Word of God.' We now have people across the globe memorising Scriptures and quoting them back to God every day in prayers reminding this forgetful old Father in heaven of the things He may have said in the past. It would funny if it wasn't so serious!

This kind of teaching leads to memorised prayers and Scriptures becoming daily rituals. Not too different to the incantations of the occult, in fact. That's not a relationship – that's witchcraft. That kind of prayer is not the spontaneous, intimate, personal dialogue between two personalities - it is a tool, a formula or a weapon.

I hear someone protest, *"But didn't Jesus use Scripture this way?"* Good question. Did He? The answer is simple: absolutely not! So many people have taken Jesus' encounter with Satan in the wilderness and built all kinds of interesting and complicated theologies from a simple story.

To begin with, Jesus was not using Scripture in some magical way like a sorcerer might use an incantation. He was simply reminding the prince of demons of truths which Satan already knew. Do you think that was the first encounter Satan had with the Scriptures? Not at all. He knew all those Scriptures as well as Jesus. That's why Jesus quoted them - he was giving His adversary a touch of reality - reminding him of some facts of life which Satan already knew.

Now, as for this being used as a model for praying the Scriptures or quoting the Bible in prayer, that is nonsense. Jesus was not praying. Jesus was not talking to His father. There is no evidence at all that Jesus quoted Scripture back to God in prayer.

Yet there are thousands of people who have developed elaborate methods of praying and standing on certain Scriptures in prayer which they claim has some Biblical precedent. I'm afraid I can't see that. Not only is this kind of prayer wrong and impersonal and an abuse of the privilege of prayer, but it's also boring in the extreme. Can you imagine the quality of your relationship with your wife or husband or friend if every time you saw them, they recited the same words over and over again to you, or read from a book which you actually wrote and already know off by heart? This is how many people talk to God. If it wasn't so sad, it would be really funny.

The kind of teaching, apart from lead millions of people astray, simply creates an elite group within the church. The ones who supposedly know how to pray and how get God to do things. They become separated from the rest of the church who are the boring masses who don't know much at all and have no power.

2 Chronicles 7:14 is all about relationship! *"If my people who are called my name will humble themselves and pray and seek my face …* Read that again! This is all about relationship! Prayer is a means by which we communicate with a personal, living, all-powerful God. Our position in prayer is always humility. We humble ourselves before the One Who holds all the power and all the answers and all the keys to the Kingdom of God. He is God and we are not!

That is as true the first day we began journey as a Christian as it will be on the last day. It doesn't matter how much we learn and know about God. It doesn't matter how many prayer seminars we attend. It doesn't matter how strong our faith is and what we are 'believing God for' today - He is still God, and we are not, and at times He will act in ways which we neither understand nor enjoy.

I know all the positive affirmation stuff. I know how important it is for us to know who we are in Christ. I have preached that to thousands of people for over 40 years. We are not to have a spirit of fear and timidity.

We are children of the King and we have the presence of the Lord Himself within us. All that is true. Yet none of that changes the fact that when we come to God in prayer, we come as broken, contrite, humble servants, always acknowledging Him to be our sovereign God and confessing our total dependence upon Him every moment of every day.

Humility is the key to the throne room - always has been, always will be. We can name and claim all the promises we like; we can quote Scripture until the cows come home; it won't change the fact the God is God, and we are not, and we must approach Him in humility.

Too many people confuse being bold *for* God with being bold *in the presence of* God.

Being bold *for* God is wonderful. We have many of exhortations in the Bible to be bold for God as we forcefully lay hold of the Kingdom of God and march against the enemy. But where does it say that we are to be bold in the presence of God? Nowhere. We are to bow in awe, humility, submission, and reverence before our sovereign God, and in His grace and mercy He exalts us in Christ and empowers us to be His bold warriors. We are to always be humble in the presence of our God and bold in our ministry for God.

That is so clear in the Bible and yet there is a strand of teaching which is growing rapidly across the world which effectively says that we are to be bold in the presence of God too. It effectively makes us like God. If only we have the faith to believe and if only we learn how to pray the right prayers and use the right words and stand on the right Scriptures, then things will really happen.

What did Jesus have to say to the people who prayed the right prayers and had the right brand of faith and heard from God in a special way that no one else could hear? Read Matthew 23 and find out. He called them *'a brood of vipers.'* He said they were like *'white-washed tombs'* ... looking great on the outside but full of death on the inside.

That elitist spirit of the Pharisee is still alive and well today. It is really hard for us to remain humble when we are given such a wonderful gift from God; when He pours out His love and grace and mercy and wisdom upon us, it is so easy for us to start thinking *we* did something to make this happen. This all comes back to an understanding of the partnership into which God has called us.

We have explored the various 'if … then' scenarios in this book and have been reminded of our responsibility to help advance the Kingdom of God. It is vitally important for us to know that God has called us and equipped us to minister in His power and strength and to have faith in His ability to work through us. So, aren't I saying the same thing as the word of faith teachers when I say if we do something then God will do something and if we don't then He won't? Good question.

The simplest answer I can give is this and I want you to really understand what I am saying here: there is a huge difference between saying, "*If I don't do this then God **won't** do that …*" and saying, "*If I don't do this then God **can't** do that.*"

We need to allow the Holy Spirit to reveal to our hearts that God is sovereign and yet He is committed to a partnership and that is why He chooses to work through us. It is an awesome privilege and responsibility and there will be heaps of things that God will not do without us. But to take that truth one step further and say that He is *unable* to do it without us, is to venture into heresy.

The difference, in what you hear reads in this book and what is being preached under the word of faith banner all over the world is that everything you read here is built upon the foundation of God's grace and a constant recognition of His sovereignty. We must never forget those powerful words of the Apostle Paul:

> "*By the grace of God I am what I am, and his grace to me was not without effect. No, I worked harder than all of them - yet not I, but the grace of God that was with me.*" (1 Corinthians 15:10)

As I warned at the beginning of this book, unless we have a firm grasp on the grace of God and the sovereignty of God then any exhortation concerning our place in the scheme of things is open to being distorted into a religious work. This verse was as true the first day I stumbled to walk in the kingdom of God as it is fifty years later after I have grown in my Christian faith and my understanding of God. Embracing the truth of that verse will help keep us humble in the presence of God. So too with this powerful verse:

> "Not by might nor by power, but by my Spirit," says the LORD Almighty. (Zechariah 4:6)

In essence, this verse says that nothing at all is accomplished by human effort - nothing of any significance, anyway. It is only that which the Spirit of God instigates and empowers that is effective in God's kingdom. Even Jesus when He ministered among us as a man said, "I only do what I see the Father doing." He also said, "I only speak the words he gives me." What an incredible picture that give us of humility, submission, surrender, dependence, and accountability. What a great role-model for us.

I want to leave it here for now and encourage you to review this chapter before reading on. This is really important for us all to grasp. Ask God to show you what He wants to teach you and discard the rest. There is so much false teaching out there about prayer and I am convinced the enemy of God is behind it all because I have seen the result: frustrated, defeated, discouraged disciples who pray less and less because the 'results' don't match what so many preachers are shouting at them every week!

It is my prayer that when you have finished this book, you will be forever free from any and all of that demonic teaching which would seek to rob you of the power and importance of prayer.

CHAPTER THIRTEEN
The Privilege of Prayer

As we continue to explore this important issue of prayer, I want to expand my cautionary warning from the previous chapter. If you are one who has enjoyed the blessings of God in answer to prayer in some area of your life and you want to tell the whole world about it - please be careful what you say and to whom - lest you take your personal encounter with God and make it prescriptive for all people. There are certainly times when you should declare the wonderful works of God to all who want to hear. But then there are those times, like Mary, the mother of Jesus, when you should just "ponder these things in your heart." Either way, just be careful that you don't try to take credit for something <u>God</u> has done.

If God says, 'yes' to your prayer, it was not the quality of your prayer that brought the answer; it was not the words you used or the Scriptures you 'prayed' and 'stood' on; it was not your boldness or passion or volume or the language with which you prayed. It was the grace of God in harmony with the will of God which brought the answer to that prayer and that's a very special and very personal encounter for which you should be incredibly grateful and humbled.

In Jesus name, I beg you not to race out to a brother or sister and tell them that if they do what you just did – then they too can experience the same answer to prayer. **Prayer is not the currency with which we buy something from God.** There is no money-back guarantee that God will answer you the same way every time. He will always answer, in His time, but there is nothing we can do to guarantee a 'yes' every time.

Prayer is not a 'method' we learn to extract the blessings of God. Prayer is not a program or a tool. Prayer is not even a ministry in and of itself. In fact, even the term 'Prayer Meeting' is a very misleading term. It conjures up the idea that prayer is the purpose of the meeting, the end result.

That is like coming together as leaders of a church or directors of a company and looking at the agenda and finding only one word there: TALK. That isn't an agenda. You don't just gather to talk. Talking is not the purpose of the meeting. What a waste of time. You gather to talk *about* something. There is another purpose to be achieved. Talking is merely the means by which you achieve that purpose.

The same is true of prayer. Prayer is not the focus of any meeting. We don't meet for prayer. Prayer is not the goal. Prayer is not the end. Prayer is the means to a far greater end: The Transformation of your city, and your nation, through the transformation of your life, which produces a burden to pray more!

Now I am not suggesting you change your vocabulary and terms because of this: but I do want to remind you of the importance of what I am saying and heed the warning that prayer can become an end in itself, and even an idol.

Of course, there are a few things we can learn about prayer which may help us understand this wonderful gift. But as with human speech, the only way we really learn anything is by doing it. You cannot learn to speak by looking at pictures in a book or by attending a seminar. You learn to speak by speaking.

The best way to learn to pray is by praying and, like the disciples, we too will ask the Lord to *'teach us to pray.'* In response to that question Jesus uttered those precious words which we named The Lord's Prayer. One of the most important and foundational statements in that prayer are the words, *"Thy will be done ..."* That must be our attitude from beginning to end in our prayer times.

Even our most passionate, faith-fuelled prayers must, in the final analysis, be laid on the altar of *"Your will, O Lord, not mine be done."* Those are the words which Jesus Himself cried out to the Father in the garden of tears and pain before going to His death and it is that same broken, contrite, submissive spirit which should permeate all that we say and do and pray.

Was Jesus a wimp with no faith in God? I think not. In fact, often it is those with the most faith who can accept God's will even when it is the exact opposite to what they may have prayed. Some would suggest that you cannot entertain the idea of God saying no when you pray because that will rob you of your faith.

In fact, the morning I was drafting this chapter, I clicked on a video on Facebook of one of these word of faith preachers, just out of curiosity - only to hear this brother yelling at me and pointing his finger at the camera as he said these exact words with incredible passion:

> *"If you want God to do something you have to visualise the outcome … focus on the reality of that for which you are praying … and don't allow anything or anyone to stop you from believing for that which you pray. Don't let those wishy-washy 'if it be thy will' people sap you of your faith. You enter that throne room by the blood of Jesus, and you look your Father in the eye and you claim that which belongs to you with confidence, with boldness and with the assurance it will come to pass!"*

I confess I was caught off-guard because I became quite upset by this brief video - especially when I noticed it had received over two million views around the world! I wasn't just upset that someone would preach that, I think I was recalling all the times I had cried out to God, and He said 'no.' I think I was recalling the people who had died right before my eyes whilst I was praying for their healing. I think I was recalling how I felt the day I saw that tiny white coffin lowered into the ground during my first funeral for a baby born dead - at the end of a text-book pregnancy - and nine months of sincere prayer; I am sure I was remembering the thousands of people in the world who were praying for healing for our baby granddaughter Lyla, only to see her earthly journey end after only 14 months. I was upset on behalf of the millions of people who were listening to this well-meaning brother who may follow his advice now and barge into the throne room of God like he suggested and demand things from our heavenly Father which, in His grace He may just give them, but I know that to many of them the answer will be 'no.'

My heart ached for those people. I grieved for the ones who had nowhere to go when God said 'no' because their theology and their understanding of prayer did not allow room for God to ever say 'no.' I have sat with many brothers and sisters like that who are broken and destitute because their faith in God's ability to answer their prayer had become greater than their faith in God Himself. Please don't skip over that sentence! Let me make it really clear this time:

It is possible for you to have more faith in God's ability to answer your prayer than you have in God Himself.

You see, this really is all about relationship, not results. It is about trusting a Person Whom we know really well. It is about coming before a loving, gracious, but sovereign God with the kind of faith that can on the one hand ask for everything and yet also be satisfied with nothing, if that is what God chooses to give. It seems incredibly complex, yet it's incredibly simple.

When we cannot understand the spiritual realm and the true purpose of prayer, we too often race into false teaching. Prayer is so important, but it is <u>God</u> who works to perform His will, and so we get the idea that we must generate enough prayer to get Him going and we make up theories as to why this prayer didn't produce the answer, but the next one might.

I don't believe the word of faith people have much faith at all because they are not willing to even entertain the idea that God would not want to give them what they are praying for. They would say that as soon as you even think about the possibility of God not answering your prayer with a resounding 'Yes!' ... you cut off the force behind your faith. That is not faith! That is blind, stubborn determination to get your own way. We discipline our children for such arrogance but then exalt supposedly mature Christians to the status of super-saint when they exhibit the same arrogance in the presence of God. In Jesus name, listen to what I am really saying here. I think we all need more faith. I think we settle for far less than God wants for us.

I think unbelief is a huge problem among Christians today. I think we need to stand on the rock and proclaim the truth of who we are in Christ. All this is true. However, our position before God must ALWAYS be one of humility, servitude, submission, obedience, and trust. We are told to ask God for anything, and He will grant it according to His will. He is sovereign and He knows best and there will be times when we must wait a long time for Him to grant our request.

I know of some people waited decades for the answer. There will be other times God will grant our request the moment we pray. Then there are the times when He clearly says a firm 'no' and often without any reason or explanation. He is able to do that, because He is God, and we are not.

By all means, let's ask God to increase our faith. Let's be more diligent in seeking the face of God in prayer. Let's ask the Lord to help us in our unbelief. But let's ask Him for the kind of faith that can handle those times when He says 'no.' That is the test of real faith.

Anyone can believe in a God who always says 'yes.' How easy is that? Only those who have taken the time in prayer to build a close, intimate relationship with God; only those who really know Him, will remain strong in their faith when the answer to their prayer is not what they hoped for. When we know God and trust God, His 'no' is as powerful as His 'yes.'

I plead with you, don't just accept everything you are reading because it resonates with your anti 'word of faith' theology; or don't sit there with a fire in your belly because I have trampled all over your faith and your beliefs, as you frantically gather all the references and material you can to prove me wrong and ease your conscience. Regardless of how you respond to what I have written here, you need to go to <u>God</u> and no one else. Seek His face alone and ask Him to confirm His Word in what I have written. Just make sure you are ready to receive whatever He gives you at that point. Don't ask Him to confirm His Word if you are not willing to accept it and then act on it.

CHAPTER FOURTEEN
Checking our Foundations

Before we venture any further into this extended teaching based on 2 Chronicles 7:14, I need to take some time to make sure that our foundation is secure. If you imagine this book is a building project which takes many months to complete, then we need to make sure we are building on a really solid foundation. That is vital when building a house and even more so when our project is a multi-storey building. Using that analogy, when finished, this 'building' will be 21 storeys high (and over 80,000 words!). Unless you have a really strong foundation to lay all of that teaching on, disaster awaits you.

That foundation, as I stressed at the beginning of this book, is grace. God's grace is the foundation of the Christian faith and the key to life. The grace of God reveals the essence of God in His dealings with us, which is why I have joined the Apostle Paul many times already in this book already in declaring, *"By the grace of God I am what I am ..."* I also affirm that by the grace of God you are what you are, and the church is what it is today by God's grace. Let's read that whole verse again:

> *"By the grace of God I am what I am, and His grace to me was not without effect. No, I worked harder than all of them - yet not I, but the grace of God that was with me." (1 Corinthians 15:10)*

Without a firm foundation in God's grace, without a crystal-clear understanding of God's grace, we will not be able to handle the exhortations contained in 2 Chronicles 7:14. They will be too heavy, and we will find that our foundation will crack and the whole structure will eventually fall in a heap and take us down with it.

This was true in Jesus' day and in Paul's day. That is why they preached and demonstrated the grace of God as much as they did. It was a safeguard, a foundation, and the backdrop for all the 'hard words' they also preached.

If you have really engaged with this book thus far, you will have to agree that it has contained a few hard words already – some of which will offend and bruise and discourage those whose faith is not firmly grounded in God's grace. Unless your personal relationship with God is secure in your mind and heart (and that cannot happen without a solid understanding of His grace) then I guarantee that your foundation will crack under the load of this teaching (perhaps it has already?). This is why Paul issued this warning to the Church in Philippi:

> *"It is no trouble for me to write the same things to you again, it is a safeguard for you." (Philippians 3:1)*

The "same things" Paul was referring to here is the foundation of God's grace which he preached over and over and over again. He knew how easy it was for us be lured away from the bedrock of the true gospel as our foundation is eroded by the enemy and false teaching. Jesus faced this same dynamic with the first disciples. Let's read these challenging words from our Lord:

> *"Many of Jesus' disciples said, "This is a hard teaching. Who can accept it?" … Jesus said to them, "Does this offend you? … The Spirit gives life; the flesh counts for nothing. The words I have spoken to you are spirit and they are life. Yet there are some of you who do not believe … From this time many of his disciples turned back and no longer followed him. "You do not want to leave too, do you?" Jesus asked the Twelve." (John 6:60-67)*

The hard teaching Jesus was giving them at that point was similar to the hard teaching coming in this book. What He was saying effectively was that unless those seeds are planted in the seedbed of God's grace - deep in our spirit - they will wither and die quickly or be misinterpreted by our fallen flesh and may even damage us.

I received an email recently from someone who connects with my teaching online each week from South Africa. It was a very transparent and brutally honest confession from a very sincere disciple of Jesus.

There were four words which were clearly written from a pit of despair, and yet they were music to my ears (and to God's ears too). Those words were, *"I can't do this."*

This person has come to the realisation that we all must come to at some point. He has reached the end of his resources, and he confesses now that he just cannot live up to the clear expectations laid out in the New Testament. He has read all the exhortations and admonitions and warnings, and he just sank in a pit of despair, because it's just too hard.

This makes perfect sense because the expectations of a sincere disciple of Jesus Christ are impossible for us to meet and until you get to the end of yourself and say, *"I can't do this;"* until you recognise that the high expectations of Scripture are way beyond your fallen flesh's ability, you have missed the whole essence of the Gospel and the Christian life.

Let's face it - we are dead at the starting gate in this race! Have you read some of the stuff in the New Testament? Have you looked at what is expected of you and me? Let me lay some of those expectations on you right now and see how you might feel in the flesh. Brace yourself.

> *"Make every effort to live in peace with all men and to be holy; without holiness no one will see the Lord." (Hebrews 12:14)*

> *"Make every effort to add to your faith goodness; and to goodness, knowledge; and to knowledge, self-control; and to self-control, perseverance; and to perseverance, godliness; and to godliness, brotherly kindness; and to brotherly kindness, love. For if you possess these qualities in increasing measure, they will keep you from being ineffective and unproductive in your knowledge of our Lord Jesus Christ." (1 Peter 1:5-8)*

> *"Be completely humble and gentle; be patient, bearing with one another in love. Make every effort to keep the unity of the Spirit through the bond of peace." (Ephesians 4:2-3)*

"Pursue righteousness, godliness, faith, love, endurance, and gentleness. Fight the good fight of the faith. Take hold of the eternal life to which you were called." (1 Timothy 6:11-12)

These are heavy expectations from Paul and Peter and the writer of Hebrews, and these are just a few samples - there are hundreds more! But they were amateurs compared to Jesus! Have a look what He dumped on us:

"For I tell you that unless your righteousness surpasses that of the Pharisees and the teachers of the law, you will certainly not enter the kingdom of heaven. You have heard that it was said to the people long ago, 'Do not murder, and anyone who murders will be subject to judgment. But I tell you that anyone who is angry with his brother will be subject to judgment ...

"You have heard that it was said, 'Do not commit adultery.' But I tell you that anyone who looks at a woman lustfully has already committed adultery with her in his heart. If your right eye causes you to sin, gouge it out and throw it away. It is better for you to lose one part of your body than for your whole body to be thrown into hell.

And if your right hand causes you to sin, cut it off and throw it away. It is better for you to lose one part of your body than for your whole body to go into hell ...

... "You have heard that it was said, 'Eye for eye, and tooth for tooth.' But I tell you, do not resist an evil person. If someone strikes you on the right cheek, turn to him the other also.

... "You have heard that it was said, 'Love your neighbour and hate your enemy.' But I tell you: Love your enemies and pray for those who persecute you, that you may be sons and daughters of your Father in heaven.

... Be perfect, therefore, as your heavenly Father is perfect. "
(Matthew 5:20-48)

All the way through His ministry, Jesus raised the bar so high that no sinful human being could ever clear it. For generation after generation the people of God had blown it.

Read the Old Testament and you will see time after time after time, how we utterly failed to meet the holy standards of God. We needed to be saved from ourselves! So, when our Saviour finally came, what did He do? He took the law of God; He took the righteous requirements of the law, and He made them even harder! He deliberately raised the bar so incredibly high in order to show us once and for all that **we can't do it.** We are totally incapable of reaching the high expectations of God!

Enter … the grace of God.

Enter … the gospel of the Lord Jesus Christ.

Enter … the Word made flesh, the incarnate Son of God.

Enter … the life death and resurrection of Jesus – gifted to us.

We could not come close to meeting the righteous requirements of God, so Jesus did it for us. He was the only human being who ever met and ever will meet those requirements … and it is His obedience, His perfect performance against the law of God, which is now credited to our account by the grace of God. Can you see why they call this 'good news'?! But wait, there's more!

The wages of sin is death and the cause-and-effect laws of the universe required that sin must be atoned for – but no longer by the blood of goats and bulls which was always only temporary in its effect - this time God ended this saga with sin once and for all when He became flesh and died on our behalf - paying the price for sin once and forever.

The holiness of God burned against all sin as the broken body of Jesus breathed its last breath on the cross. That death was also credited to our account as if it was our own death. In some mysterious, but glorious exchange in heaven, all of our sin was traded for the righteousness of Christ. But wait, there's more!

Jesus then conquered death! His resurrection to new life and victory over sin, death and Satan was then also credited to us. The Bible says that we were united with Him in His death and His resurrection so that now we are united with Him, seated at the right hand of God in His eternal kingdom!

We are citizens of the Kingdom of Heaven already! All of this came by the grace of God. The justice, mercy and grace of God were all in operation in this wonderful transaction.

Justice is when we get what we deserve ... but Jesus got what we deserved.

Mercy is when we don't get what we deserve ... and we did not have to pay the price of our sin. We were headed for an eternity outside of the presence of God, and He stepped in and saved us.

Grace is when we do get what we don't deserve and who would be arrogant enough to suggest that we deserve salvation? We are given the righteous robes of Jesus to wear as we walk into the throne room and fall at the feet of our holy, loving Heavenly Father. That is grace. That is God at work in us and for us.

Now there are countless Christians who would say 'amen' to all the above, but their concept of grace stops at conversion. They buy into the heresy which says, *"Grace gets us in the door ... but then we need to do all the rest."* That sounds fair enough, God achieved a lot in securing our salvation; it cost Him everything; the least we can do is play our part and do our bit to make all this work. There is only one problem ... **we can't do it!** Grace doesn't just get us in the door - grace empowers us to live up to the high and holy calling as a disciple of Jesus. Let's look at some Scriptures which remind us of this. The first one should be really familiar by now!

> *"By the grace of God I am what I am, and His grace to me was not without effect. No, I worked harder than all of them - yet not I, but the grace of God that was with me." (1 Corinthians 15:10)*

> *"My grace is sufficient for you, for my power is made perfect in weakness. Therefore, I will boast all the more gladly about my weaknesses, so that Christ's power may rest on me."*
> *(2 Corinthians 12:9)*

> *"You who are trying to be justified by law have been alienated from Christ; you have fallen away from grace." (Galatians 5:4)*

"But he gives us more grace. That is why Scripture says: 'God opposes the proud but gives grace to the humble.'" (James 4:6)

So, what is this grace? Many traditional commentaries and dictionaries define it as *'God's unmerited favour.'* That definition is misleading and contributes to the error of thinking that grace is that which is in operation only when we are first saved. I believe *'God's unmerited favour'* is a far better definition for mercy, not grace.

In my book, *'Amazing Grace,'* I went into great detail to explain this by putting the word's *'God's unmerited favour'* in the place of the word *'grace'* wherever it appears in the New Testament. It fits well in some verses, but it makes absolutely no sense in most verses and yet the word is the same in the Greek.

So, as I pointed out in that book, I believe a far more accurate definition for grace is *'The Empowering Presence of God.'* Test that one out in every example of 'grace' in the New Testament and they will all fit, and the verses will also come to life in an amazing way!

You may be wondering how I responded to my brother in South Africa? How do you face such clear exhortations in the New Testament which tell us what we should be doing and how we should be living? Let me tell you first what you should NOT do when you hear or read those exhortations. You should not jump back 2,000 years and put yourself on the other side of the cross. You should not read these exhortations like people would have read the commands of God under the old covenant.

These are not legalistic requirements laid out before those who desire to please God and want to escape His wrath. As a new covenant, born again believer in Christ, you cannot please God any more than He is already pleased because you stand in His grace, dressed in righteous robes of the Lord Jesus Christ. The Bible says you are in Christ, and God is very pleased with His Son – so He is pleased with you. This is not about pleasing God or earning His love or blessing.

When you understand grace; when you walk in the empowering presence of God; then you will see these exhortations and characteristics of a mature Christian in a totally different light. You will see them as promises of who you are becoming in Christ. You will see them as the goal or destiny of every believer who presses into the heart of God.

So why worry about any of them then? Why teach this stuff if these are not requirements of God? Why not just focus on the grace of God and let Him do the rest? Good question. I used to wonder that myself. The reason why I must teach the hard word and issue the strong exhortations to grow up into Christ and take responsibility for our actions is because that's what Jesus and Paul did. That's what is in the whole New Testament. Like Jesus and Paul, I have laid a foundation of God's grace upon which I can now build the rest of what I see to be the fullness of New Testament Christianity. I cannot ignore stuff that is on every second page of the New Testament. It is there for a reason. It is there to mature us, to refine us, to shape us into all that God desires for us to be.

These exhortations are given so that we know where we are headed. As Paul said so well, God's grace is meant to have an effect in us. It is meant to do more than make us feel warm and mushy inside at the thought of God loving us so much. When we understand grace as the empowering presence of God, then we can open the New Testament and read what we are empowered to do and who we are empowered to be. All these 'hard words' and admonitions are meant to do one thing and one thing only: drive us to our knees in humble submission before the God in Whose grace we stand.

When we read that wonderful list of the fruit of the Spirit in Galatians 5: love, joy, peace, patience, kindness, goodness, gentleness, and self-control - and then look in the mirror - we are not meant to crumble in despair because of our constant failure to live up to such expectations. We are not meant to see them as things we are supposed to strive to achieve. The passage itself says that these are the fruit of the Spirit of God.

So now for the magic question: How do we get it? How do we obtain or walk in or appropriate or experience this grace, this empowering presence of God? Well, you already know the answer! The opening words of 2 Chronicles 7:14 make it really clear. Humility is the key. The Bible has already told us that God opposes the proud but gives grace to the humble, and with that fuller definition of grace, we can see that key more clearly:

God opposes the proud (those who seek to achieve this calling in their own strength) **but He gives His empowering presence to the humble** (those whose No.1 priority is their personal relationship with God).

You see, as I have said in the previous chapters - this is <u>all</u> about relationship. That is the source of our power and our ability to rise to the challenge of being the mighty army of God who marches against the powers of darkness. We march on our knees; we march on our faces before God in humble adoration and submission.

We all love the story of the battle of Jehosophat in 2 Chronicles 20 when God brought a victory as the worship leaders were sent out ahead of the army. God was making a really important point that day, which is as true now as it was then. The battle belongs to the Lord and our place is in humble submission to Him at every point in our journey.

Next time you read that passage, I want you to notice something. In verse 17 the Lord tells the people through the prophetic voice to *"take up their positions"* and watch the Lord bring the victory. Have you ever wondered what that position was? I used to picture these people all standing on the edge of the mountain, weapons ready, watching the battle unfold. But I missed the very next verse after God told them to take up their positions. Verse 18 clearly shows us what that position is:

"Jehosophat bowed with his face to the ground, and all the people of Judah and Jerusalem fell down in worship before the LORD."
(2 Chronicles 20:18)

The empowering presence of God was unleashed that day as the people humbled themselves before the Lord. We focus on the worship band out the front and think that was what brought the victory. That is only partly true. Without the humble submission of the people of God, they would never have agreed to send the worshippers out in front – that would seem incomprehensible to the battle-hardened men of Judah. Humility released the grace of God. Humility unleashed the power of God and victory came.

I will therefore continue to preach, teach and write those hard words. I will continue to bring that mirror up before us as we look into the faces of our enemies - those enemies which lurk within our own hearts. Enemies pride, fear, laziness, selfishness, and all the rest.

We cannot ignore those enemies, they are real. We cannot ignore the exhortations of God, they are real. We cannot be complacent about the thousands of people slipping into eternity each day while we play 'nice to be nice' church games once or twice a week. We cannot ignore that huge credibility gap which exists when we look at the church described in the New Testament and the impact it had on society then, compared to the church of today and the impact we are *not* having on society. We must grow up into Christ and face the responsibilities of discipleship!

However, we must also be on guard at every point for religious spirits that will seduce us and entice us back into religion and performance-based righteousness! If discouragement or shame come your way as you read these hard words, then you need to realise what is happening … you are falling away from grace and the empowering presence of God is no longer the force behind your motivation to obey and serve and grow and mature.

Like Jehosophat, we need to take up our positions, humbly on our face; pressing into the heart of God every day; pursuing a personal, intimate relationship with Him as our highest priority. Only then will we see victory. Only then will we see maturity emerging in our walk with God. Only then will we live to see the day when God truly does heal our land!

CHAPTER FIFTEEN
Seeking God's Face

*"If my people, who are called by my name, will humble themselves and pray and **seek my face** and turn from their wicked ways, then I will hear from heaven, and I will forgive their sin and will heal their land." (2 Chronicles 7:14)*

Seeking the face of God is all about intimacy with God and I want to spend some time looking at this vital issue of our intimate relationship with God. I pray that He will open the eyes of your heart as you draw near to Him. Let's read this declaration of God to His people from many years ago:

"The days are coming," declares the Lord, "when I will make a new covenant with the people of Israel and with the people of Judah. It will not be like the covenant I made with their ancestors when I took them by the hand to lead them out of Egypt, because they broke my covenant, though I was a husband to them," declares the Lord.

"This is the covenant I will make with the people of Israel after that time," declares the Lord. "I will put my law in their minds and write it on their hearts. I will be their God, and they will be my people. No longer will they teach their neighbour, or say to one another, 'Know the Lord,' because they will all know me, from the least of them to the greatest," declares the Lord. "For I will forgive their wickedness and will remember their sins no more." (Jeremiah 31:31-34)

Being a Christian is all about our relationship with God. It is not what we know *about* God that defines our faith. We can know a great deal *about* God without having much personal knowledge *of* God Himself.

"You believe that there is one God. Good! Even the demons believe that - and shudder." (James 2:19)

Knowing stuff about God makes us no better than the demons! This is also not primarily about religious works and disciplines (baptism, communion, worship, prayer, Bible reading, etc.), however valuable they may be.

Nor is it primarily about good behaviour, about holy living, although that too is important. Like the Pharisees, we can know a great deal about godliness without possessing much knowledge of God as a Person.

The essence of New Covenant living is knowing God personally. This is what distinguished it from the Old Covenant: "*They will all know Me, from the least of them to the greatest.*" It is about having a genuine relationship with the living, present God and it's not supposed to be something abstract or theoretical, but an ongoing experiential reality affecting every part of our being. It is not just about head-knowledge, but deep, sincere heart-and-soul-and-spirit-knowledge.

Do you know God personally, or is He just a vague acquaintance whose book you have read? I read Nelson Mandella's lengthy autobiography and so now I know a lot about this incredible man – but I never met him and never knew him personally.

It seems that many people are happy to talk about knowing God without there being a deep, daily reality behind their words. What a tragedy that being a Christian has so often been reduced to accepting a few truths and following a few rules. As Jeanne Guyon wrote three hundred years ago:

> "*What inexpressible damage new Christians - for that matter, most Christians - have suffered because of the loss of an inner, spiritual relationship with God.*"

Jesus made it very clear that our relationship with God was at the heart of everything:

> "*Now this is eternal life: that they know you, the only true God, and Jesus Christ, whom you have sent.*" (John 17:3)

Long before Jesus even arrived on earth, knowing God was always commended and highly valued.

> *"Let not the wise man boast of his wisdom or the strong man boast of his strength, or the rich man boast of his riches, but let him who boasts boast about this: that he understands and knows Me." (Jeremiah 9:23-24)*

What do we boast about? Whatever the depth (or shallowness) of our personal experience of God, we can always know Him better. In this life we shall always only know God in part, but Paul's prayer for the Ephesian believers should also be our daily prayer for ourselves:

> *"I keep asking that the God of our Lord Jesus Christ, the glorious Father, may give you the Spirit of wisdom and revelation, so that you may know Him better." (Ephesians 1:17)*

There is certainly no greater pursuit than the pursuit of a deeper relationship with God and nothing should have a higher priority in our lives. James Packer summarises it like this:

> *"What were we made for? To know God. What aim should we set ourselves in life? To know God. What is the 'eternal life' that Jesus gives? Knowledge of God. What is the best thing in life, bringing more joy, delight, and contentment, than anything else? Knowing God. What, of all the states God ever sees man in, gives Him most pleasure? Knowing Him."*

As Henri Nouwen once put it, "*The only thing that really matters is your relationship with God.*" But what kind of relationship can we expect to have with the Lord God Almighty? How are we supposed to relate to the infinite, awesome, holy King of the universe Who reigns in glory and majesty? The answer to this question is really quite astounding. We would perhaps expect that God's 'wholly otherness' would create an uncrossable canyon between the us and our God, and that we could only know Him at a distance. But that isn't how we are meant to relate to Him at all.

God's amazing grace has completely bridged the gulf between us, and He now calls us His friends. On His way to Gethsemane, Jesus made this startling revelation:

> *"I no longer call you servants, because a servant does not know his master's business. Instead, I have called you friends, for everything that I learned from My Father I have made known to you."* (John 15:15)

Even under the Old Covenant, it was possible to know God as a friend. Three times in Scripture, Abraham is described as God's friend. Similarly, it was said of Moses that the Lord would speak to him face to face, as a man speaks with his friend. And in the dark days of his suffering and apparent abandonment by God, Job exclaimed, "*Oh, for the days when I was in my prime, when God's intimate friendship blessed my house!*"

How much more should we, who have received the Holy Spirit under the New Covenant, know God as our intimate friend! The King of kings wants us to relate to Him as friends and not just as His subjects. As our friend, we know He is committed to us; He is on our side; He wants the very best for us; He sticks with us through thick and thin. We can relax in His presence and be open with Him because we can trust Him, knowing that He is *for* us. He wants us to share our whole lives with Him and for us to do everything in partnership with Him. He desires to always be our companion and partner in everything we do.

Not only is God described as our 'friend' in the Scriptures, but He is also portrayed as our 'husband' or a bridegroom. Jesus referred to Himself as the bridegroom and His return is described in the book of Revelation as the wedding of the Lamb.

Jesus is returning as the bridegroom for His beautiful bride. Indeed, Paul sees human marriage as but a reflection of the profound mystery of the union between Christ and His church. In the uniting of man and wife lies an illustration of the intimacy of the close relationship God desires to have with His people. There are hints of this even under the Old Covenant.

In words very similar to those of Jesus above - the Lord says through Hosea to His people, "*You will call Me 'my husband'; you will no longer call Me 'my master.'*"

Similarly, He promises through Isaiah, "*As a young man marries a maiden, so will your Builder marry you; as a bridegroom rejoices over his bride, so will your God rejoice over you.*"

We, the church, are the bride of the King of kings. We can relate to Him as His bride and not just as His subjects. The relationship between husband and wife is an intimate one; everything is shared; it is a relationship of oneness and love.

This is the kind of relationship God wants us to have with Him. He desires to draw us into the depths of His heart. As well as being friends of the Lord and the bride of the Lamb, we are also referred to as God's children.

> "*How great is the love the Father has lavished on us, that we should be called children of God! And that is what we are!*"
> (1 John 1:3)

Under the Old Covenant, the Lord declared, "*I am Israel's father, and Ephraim is my firstborn son.*" And the Psalmist proclaimed, "*As a father has compassion on his children, so the Lord has compassion on those who fear Him.*"

But Jesus revealed a new closeness to this relationship. He knew God as His personal loving heavenly Father. You will remember the voice which came from heaven at His baptism and His transfiguration: "*This is my Son, whom I love; with Him I am well pleased.*" Jesus also used the Aramaic word *Abba* - the word of intimacy from child to father - to refer to the Almighty God, and this was a revolutionary departure for the Jews.

The astounding fact is that, like Jesus, we too can know God as Abba, father, 'daddy,' by His Spirit Whom we have received. We, too, can have the same depth of relationship with God that Jesus had as a man.

We, too, can call the Most High God our 'dad.' Just before His arrest, Jesus prayed to His Father for us:

"I have made You known to them, and will continue to make You known in order that the love You have for Me may be in them." (John 17:26)

We are God's beloved children and so we can know the same kind of relationship with our heavenly Father that Jesus did. We are children of the King. We can relate to Him as His children and not just as His loyal subjects. Our relationship with God should be like that of a small child who delights in being with his or her father.

Not many of us, I think, would ever naturally say that we have truly known God personally. The words imply a definiteness and matter-of-factness of experience to which most of us, if we are honest, have to admit we are still strangers. And yet the expectation of Jesus and of all the New Covenant prophecies is precisely the opposite: that we would not only know God, but that we would know Him as our closest friend, the lover of our souls and our loving Father. Sadly however, if asked, *'Who is your best friend?* – not too many of us would naturally respond with the answer, *'God.'*

Are we willing to lay down other goals in our lives in order to pursue the highest goal of all: developing and deepening our intimacy with God until we can truly say that He is our closest friend and confidant; until we are captivated and absorbed by Him and passionately in love with Him? For this assuredly is our primary calling: to love God.

"Love the Lord your God with all your heart and with all your soul and with all your mind and with all your strength." (Matthew 22:37)

This is the first and greatest commandment. This is an all-encompassing, radical type of love, isn't it? I wonder how our lives would be if we truly pursued this goal more than any other in our lives and in our Churches?

There are Christian Churches with many different emphases: worship, prayer, preaching, pastoral care, healing, evangelism, care of the poor, etc. But only rarely does one come across a church that explicitly gives the highest priority to loving God - even though it's the first and greatest commandment!

Perhaps equally revealing is the fact that none of the ancient creeds or confessions of faith (nor indeed the modern "doctrinal statements") contain any mention of what is really the first evidence of genuine Christian discipleship: our love for God.

If we truly experienced the Lord's extravagant love for us, then our hearts would respond in love. For it's our experience of His love for us that causes us to love Him in response. We love God because He first loved us.

A. W. Tozer expressed it well:

> "Perceiving, as other mortals have not perceived, the burning love of God, the Christian gives God love for love. He cannot help it. Certainly, it is not the fruit of labour. Having seen the love of God, his own heart leaps in response. His heart is drawn out of him and lost in God's immensity. This dynamic of love responding to love should be at the very heart of the expression of our faith.

The Apostle Peter also gave us these profound words:

> "Though you have not seen Him, you love Him," the apostle Peter wrote, "and even though you do not see Him now, you believe in Him and are filled with an inexpressible and glorious joy." (1 Peter 1:8)

In my book, 'This is Love,' I have explored something of the depth of God's amazing love for us. But what should we expect our love for God to look like?

Surely it should look like the love we have for a close friend, the love of a husband and wife for each other and the love of a child for his or her father.

Each of these human relationships at best is but a weak reflection of what we can experience in our relationship with God, but the affection and fondness, the attraction and desire, and the devotion and commitment that characterise human love relationships, at the very least, should be present in our relationship with God.

There should be a deep emotional reality in our relationship with God. The Ephesian Christians used to be radically in love with Jesus, but the Lord exposed their hearts with these painful words:

> *"Yet I hold this against you: You have forsaken your*
> *first love. Remember the height from which you have fallen!"*
> *(Revelation 2:4-5)*

How many of us have lost our first love for God? You may remember what it was like when you first experienced God's love for you personally: how it eclipsed everything else in your life. How has your love for the Lord fared since that day?

One of the saddest things is that when the love of a new believer fades over time - this is considered acceptable. Of course, our initial love is immature, but, like the love between husband and wife, its depth should actually increase, not decrease, as it matures.

If your love for God is not growing stronger and deeper, then it will grow cold.

Those who do not press on in pursuit of the breadth, length, height and depth of God, will eventually become bored with their faith. Their shallow understanding will no longer capture their imagination, much less inflame their passion.

God created us to have a passionate, committed relationship with Him. But, so often, we replace service for relationship, focussing more on what we *do for* God than on loving Him personally.

Do you remember what the Apostle Paul wrote to the Christians in Corinth? He said any kind of ministry or service without love is worthless. 'Doing our duty" for God is totally absent from the New Testament, yet for many of us, much of what we do is out of sense of duty rather than as a love-response to God's grace and love towards us. It's not our work and achievements that warm and thrill the heart of God, but our love for Him. He is more interested in the attitude of our hearts towards Him than in the work we do for Him.

The only true success is to know Him better. Our fellowship with God should always be central. Then our 'ministry' will flow out of the love relationship we have with Him. If we are not careful, we may find that we place the ministry God has given us above our relationship with Him. This is, of course, idolatry and a form of spiritual adultery, but sadly, it's common among Christians, especially those in leadership.

Do we get more excited about God Himself or about the things we do for God? Are we more concerned about the 'success' of our ministry, what people think of us, and our status as ministers of the Gospel, than we are about how well we are connecting with God personally? Often our busyness keeps us from drawing near to Him, effectively separating us from the experience of His loving presence. We must seek to abide in Him above all else. Maybe, however, for you it is not service that takes the place of relationship, but the pursuit of knowledge.

> "Knowledge puffs up, but love builds up. The man who thinks he knows something does not yet know as he ought to know. But the man who loves God is known by God." (1 Corinthians 8:1)

Some of us love gaining knowledge about God more than loving God Himself. We behave as though it is more important to understand God than to know God. But if we wait until we understand everything about God before offering Him our devotion, we will never know Him. Our passion to know God, in humble dependence on Him, has to exceed our passion to understand everything about Him.

Some people place a higher value on studying the Bible than on developing a relationship with God, loving the 'book of the Lord' more than the 'Lord of the book'. Hear again the words of Jesus to the Pharisees – the spiritual leaders of their day:

> *"You have never heard His voice nor seen His form, nor does His word dwell in you, for you do not believe the one He sent. You diligently study the Scriptures because you think that by them you possess eternal life. These are the Scriptures that testify about Me, yet you refuse to come to Me to have life." (John 5:37-40)*

Studying Scripture does not guarantee a personal relationship with God. This is because Spiritual truth is discerned not only through the application of our intellect, but through the work of the Holy Spirit in our spirit. It is not intelligence and education that is required (the Bible itself suggests that sometimes these are more of a hindrance than a help), but humility and *"coming to Him."* What we think, is very important. Our thoughts inform our hearts. But what we think, is always only the beginning.

Until our knowledge touches and grips our heart – it is worthless. Oh, that we would pursue true 'heart knowledge' of God with the same discipline and persistence with which the scholar pursues 'head knowledge'! As Gene Edwards puts it so clearly, *"You need Christ - not in your mind, but in an all-consuming encounter."*

So, we've established the need for and the importance of seeking the face of God in intimacy … now, how do we do it? How does this happen practically in our daily lives? Good question, and I will try and answer that in the next chapter. Until then, take the time to review what I have shared here and let God speak to you.

I want to close with some words I believe came from the heart of the Father several years ago in a song I wrote which I sense He is saying to us every day in so many ways. Let the Father's heart grip your heart again as you hear His plea to you through the words God gave me almost thirty years ago:

From the Father's Heart

Why do you struggle and strive to achieve
You need to slow down for a while and believe
The power of heaven is yours for free
When you're that busy, you never receive.
Perhaps we could stroll in the garden again
I'll share your joys, your sorrow and pain
I just want to be a Father to you
Your love's more important than the work you do

My precious child, I love you,
come walk in the garden with Me
I long to be part of your journey,
to open your eyes and see
The depth of My grace and mercy,
the riches of heaven above
Come and taste My living water
and bask in My glory and love

There is so much that you'll never know
Unless I have time to help you grow
Draw aside, I'll meet you there
The secrets of my heart I share
I gave my son to bring you back home
It hurts me to see you still struggle alone
Nothing is good if it keeps you away
Turn to Me now and hear Me say:

My precious child, I love you,
come walk in the garden with Me
I long to be part of your journey,
to open your eyes and see
The depth of My grace and mercy,
the riches of heaven above
Come and taste My living water
and bask in My glory and love

© 1996 Robert Griffith

CHAPTER SIXTEEN
Pressing Into God's Heart

In the previous chapter, we began to explore the issue of seeking the face of God or intimacy with God. It can be a challenging issue because it hits at the heart of our Christian faith. It separates the genuine from the fraud. It exposes religion as it masquerades as relationship. We can only fake a genuine personal relationship with God for a short time - sooner or later we are forced to come to terms with this issue of intimacy with God.

In that chapter, I believe I established the importance of intimacy with God and so now I want to explore how we can deepen our relationship with God, get to know Him better and love Him more deeply. Firstly, we need to decide that it matters enough to us that we are actually going to do something about it. The first step toward experiencing intimacy with God is our decision to pursue Him more than we pursue other things such as happiness and success in this life.

To really find and embrace God, our passion to know Him must exceed all other passions. We must desire Him more than we desire a new house; a better friend; relief from our grief and loneliness; solutions to our problems; answers to our questions. We need to desire Him more than we desire becoming a better person; feeling happy; or even enjoying good health. God longs to be known by us far more than we long to know Him. He is relentlessly committed to working in our hearts until our passion to know Him becomes stronger than all our other passions.

However, desiring something isn't really enough, you need to make every effort to draw near to God. More than bearing fruit, your call must be to know the Lord. If you seek Him, you will always find Him. He is always near to those who draw near. Many want to enjoy His presence, but only a few really draw near. You must do more than *want* Him: you must *seek* Him. This is part of your call as a Christian. There is no higher purpose. Your victory will be proportional to your seeking.

You will always be as close to God as you truly want to be. Your victory in life will align with your desire for God. God is most available to those who are most available to Him. In other words, the ones who truly find Him are those who truly seek Him with all their heart.

In reality, the Bible is just one long invitation to come to God. From God calling to Adam and Eve in the garden in Genesis to the Spirit and the Bride saying "Come!" in Revelation - and on every page in between - God entreats us to seek Him, to come close to Him, to draw near to Him.

Through Moses:

"If you seek the Lord your God, you will find Him if you look for Him with all your heart and with all your soul." (Deuteronomy 4:9)

Through Isaiah:

"Come, all you who are thirsty, come to the waters; and you who have no money, come, buy and eat! Come, buy wine and milk without money and without cost." (Isaiah 55:1)

Through Hosea:

"Seek the Lord until He comes." (Hosea 10:12)

Through James:

"Draw near to God and He will draw near to you." (James 4:8)

Through Jesus:

"Come to Me, all you who are weary and burdened, and I will give you rest... If anyone is thirsty, let him come to Me and drink ... Here I am! I stand at the door and knock. If anyone hears My voice and opens the door, I will come in and eat with him, and he with Me." (Matthew 11:28; John 7:37; Revelation 3:20)

In order to get to know God better, we need to give time to Him. When we really want to develop relationships with our friends, with our husband or wife, with our parents or with our children, we set aside time to do so.

Indeed, we may talk about spending 'quality time' with someone when we want to work on our relationship with them: that means, time spent with someone alone with no agenda and no distractions. God wants to spend quality time with us, time when He has our undivided attention. Mary, the sister of Lazarus, understood this:

> *"As Jesus and His disciples were on their way, He came to a village where a woman named Martha opened her home to Him. She had a sister called Mary, who sat at the Lord's feet listening to what He said. But Martha was distracted by all the preparations that had to be made. She came to Him and asked, "Lord, don't you care that my sister has left me to do the work by myself? Tell her to help me!" "Martha, Martha," the Lord answered, "you are worried and upset about many things, but only one thing is needed. Mary has chosen what is better, and it will not be taken away from her." (Luke 10:38-42)*

Mary chose to spend quality time with Jesus and refused to be distracted; Martha chose not to spend time with Him. Jesus said that Mary had chosen better that day. Later, we see Mary express her devotion to Jesus in a most extravagant way, pouring a bottle of expensive perfume over Him. Again, Jesus commends her action and invites us to learn from Mary and spend time with Him as she did, letting Him change us by that encounter.

How much do you value spending time with the Lord? Does the idea of being with Him fill you with expectation and joy as it did Mary? Given how incredibly wonderful God is, it is somewhat astonishing how little time many of us spend on deepening our relationship with Him. When a young man and young woman are courting, only things over which they have no control will keep them apart. If we let God captivate our heart with His love, then we too will desire to draw near to Him above anything else.

As always, Jesus is our primary role model here. The gospels record various occasions when Jesus Himself withdrew to places of solitude to spend time with His Father:

"Very early in the morning, while it was still dark, Jesus got up, left the house and went off to a solitary place, where He prayed." (Mark 1:35)

"After He had dismissed the crowd, He went up on a mountainside by Himself to pray. When evening came, He was there alone." (Matthew 14:23)

"Jesus often withdrew to lonely places and prayed." (Luke 5:16)

If this was part of the rhythm of life for Jesus, how much more do we need to build it into the rhythm of our lives too? Are we willing to invest time in our relationship with God? Western society is so goal-oriented, in contrast to the more relationship-oriented cultures of much of the rest of the world. We often find it hard (especially perhaps for men) to invest adequate time in developing deep human relationships, let alone deepening our relationship with God. A Filipino description of Westerners I once read refers to us as, *"people with gods on their wrists."*

Giving time to just being with God, to just being in His presence, is in conflict with the values of the world in which we live. Many would tell us we are wasting time drawing aside from the world to spend time with an invisible God. We may need to make some tough decisions to do this. Spending time with God is important - indeed it's of crucial importance to the way we live - but it never seems urgent to most of us.

As a result, we find it easy to postpone it or delay it indefinitely so that it never happens. But the window of opportunity is now. Isaiah says, *"Seek the Lord while he may be found; call on Him while He is near."* We need to 'seize the day' before the years pass us by and we miss sharing the very best days of our lives with God.

Most of us will need to plan in order to give time to communion and fellowship with God. We need to make practical decisions about how we use our time. We should make unbreakable appointments with God, if you like.

God will not force us to spend time with Him - He longs for us to give Him time because we *want* to, not because we *should*. Our loving heavenly Father's desire to be with us is always much greater than our desire to be with Him, but He always allows us the freedom to remain distant from Him. It's our choice.

How we spend our time will reveal what we value. We can't do everything; we have to choose. So, are we choosing not to spend time with God, in favour of other activities? Or are we willing to sacrifice the unimportant, saying 'no' to some of the demands we or others place on us, in order to give time to God? How much is our relationship with God really worth to us?

What this means in practice will vary considerably according to our circumstances. For some, it may just be necessary to enter unbreakable appointments with God into our diary - and then make sure we keep those appointments. For others, it may be right to give up participation in Sunday sports in order to be with our church family as we worship, fellowship and pray together.

Others may decide that a change in employment is required. I read a story of a woman who had given up a lucrative job as an architect to become a cleaner in order to, in her own words, *"spend more time with Jesus."* In the world's eyes, her decision made no sense. In God's eyes, she chose something far greater. In our pursuit of intimacy with God, are we willing to reject many of the values of our culture? Are we willing to choose a lower 'standard of living' in order to pursue the higher 'quality of life' in close communion with our loving heavenly Father?

The most difficult problem is not finding the time to spend with God – but deciding that it's important enough to find the time. If we love the Lord with all our heart, soul, mind, and strength, then it should be reflected in our diaries and calendars! Relating to God is like any other relationship. If we relate to Him as a person, then we will develop a personal relationship with Him. The primary focus of time we spend with God must be on God Himself - on our relationship with Him - rather than on what we can do for Him or what He can do for us.

We should not be coming to Him primarily to be given orders to obey (as if we just worked for Him), or to ask Him to meet our needs and the needs of others (as if He worked for us), but rather to relate to Him deeply and profoundly as our closest friend, the lover of our souls and our heavenly Father.

Many people are content to spend some time every morning reading the Bible and praying, without ever experiencing the real presence of God. These same people would never be content to speak to one of their close friends for 30 minutes every morning without hearing the slightest response from that friend. But years of practice have taught us to be satisfied by the performance of religious duties, without the experience of God's real presence.

The Scriptures repeatedly speak of the need to be still before God and wait on Him:

> *"Be still before the Lord and wait patiently for Him."*
> *"Be still and know that I am God."*
> *"In repentance and rest is your salvation ..."*
> *"In quietness and trust is your strength ..."*
> *"Blessed are all who wait for Him!"*
> *"It is good to wait quietly for the salvation of the Lord."*

This is all about relationship, so we need not strive but just relax and be silent, becoming aware of His loving presence. God can reveal Himself to us more in one minute of quality time, than in many hours of 'distracted' time.

True intimacy is a place of transparency and vulnerability: where we receive both God's incredible, unconditional love and also His healing. Intimacy is a place of security, protection, peace, acceptance, affirmation, restoration, healing, refreshment, and renewal.

The benefits of a deep relationship with the Living God are beyond measure. We discover how true it is that we are blessed with *"every Spiritual blessing in Christ."* It's as we draw near to God that we find out how wonderful He really is.

It's as we enter into His presence that we discover for ourselves His incredible unconditional love: the revelation that we are completely forgiven, fully pleasing to God, totally accepted in Christ, and deeply valued by Him.

The more we get to know God's perfect love, acceptance, and affirmation, the less we will feel that we need to meet certain standards to feel good about ourselves. No longer will we feel we need to be approved by others to feel good about ourselves; no longer will we be afraid of failure or rejection because we will really know how God feels about us and that He already accepts us completely, in Christ.

Every inner need we have can be perfectly met, not because we have what it takes personally, but because God does. No material possession can bring us true joy. No human relationship can fill our hearts with divine love. No circumstance can provide us with God's peace. Only God can truly meet our needs perfectly. He gently invites us to let Him do that.

We can give our tears to God because He is our comforter. We can give our fears to God because He is our confidence. We can give our pains to God because He is our healer. We can give our stress to God because He is our peace. We can give our heaviness to God because He is our joy. We can give our loneliness to God because He is with us like no one else could ever be with us.

Spending time in God's presence should not only be the focus of our times of private devotion, but also the focus of our times of fellowship and worship. Where two or three gather together in Jesus' name, there He is, longing to meet with us.

As we come together as brothers and sisters in Christ, we should expect to meet with Him in and through each other. It should be God with whom we fellowship, not just each other. Whenever and however we meet - we should always expect to come away knowing that we have met with the Lord, and that He has deepened our relationship with Him as a result of that encounter.

Our heavenly Father invites us to walk the path of life with Him. But sometimes we go our own way, diverted by something in the distance that attracts our attention more than Him, or else we are so busy that we don't notice we're following a different road, wandering away from Him. Or we may lag behind, drawn aside by something at the side of the road, happy to enjoy the scenery where we are, while God had moved on without us.

Occasionally we run ahead, having been shown where He's taking us, not noticing that He wants us to walk more slowly or take a different route to our destination. He wants us walking with Him, side by side, listening to His voice. As Enoch and Noah were described as men who *"walked with God,"* so should we be.

The real goal is not just to find time for God but giving Him time, so He is the total focus of our attention, learning to relate to Him and experience His real presence with us throughout the day, knowing Him in the midst of any and all our activities. Jesus, as He wandered through Galilee and Judea, looked on His time as His Father's time, and so He was completely available to fulfil His Father's desires.

We too, should always be available to God. It is quite possible for us to give God half an hour every morning and an hour or two every Sundays and never really be available to Him the rest of the time.

God designed the human soul to be passionate, abandoned and committed. God intended our souls to be captured, consumed, and enthralled with Him. So, seeking God's face should come naturally! Those who have a deep love-relationship with God, value Him so much that everything else pales in significance by comparison. Charles Spurgeon expressed it very well:

"Believers love God with a deeper affection than they dare to give to any other being. They would sooner lose father and mother than part with God. They hold all earthly comforts with a loose hand, but they carry Him fast locked in their bosoms."

This has been the testimony of God's people throughout the ages:

> *"I say to the Lord, "You are my Lord; apart from you I have no good thing." (Psalm 16:2)*

> *"I have seen you in the sanctuary and beheld your power and your glory. Because your love is better than life, my lips will glorify you. I will praise you as long as I live, and in your name, I will lift up my hands. I will be fully satisfied as with the richest of foods; with singing lips my mouth will praise you."*
> *(Psalm 63:2-5)*

> *"Whom have I in heaven but You? And earth has nothing I desire besides You." (Psalm 73:25)*

> *"I consider everything a loss because of the surpassing worth of knowing Christ Jesus my Lord, for whose sake I have lost all things. I consider them garbage, that I may gain Christ and be found in him." (Philippians 3:8-9)*

Those who have truly tasted real intimacy with God, have no trouble in declaring that nothing else in life is worth anything in comparison to knowing Him. Drinking deeply from the River of Life soon removes any desire for the empty things of this world which attracted us so much before. Knowing the Lord personally and relationally, so far surpasses all other things in value, that their net worth is zero by comparison.

As we open ourselves up to experience the Lord's love, it both satisfies us deeply in a way nothing else can, and yet also makes us hunger for more. May this be the testimony of each and every one of God's children as we seek His face.

CHAPTER SEVENTEEN
The Problem of Sin

*"If my people, who are called by my name, will humble themselves and pray and seek my face and turn from their wicked ways, then I will hear from heaven, and I will forgive their **sin** and will heal their land."* (2 Chronicles 7:14)

This has been a long journey through a short verse!

... a verse which encapsulates so much truth.

... a verse which has reminded us of our responsibility in this mysterious, yet glorious partnership into which God has called each one of us.

... a verse which has re-emphasised the incredible freedom given to God's children to participate in His world-changing, nation-transforming plan ... or not.

... a verse which stresses the truth found all through the Bible, that humility is the key to the throne room of God.

... a verse which shows us yet again how our Sovereign God chooses to channel His life-changing power through the prayers, submission, and obedience of His people. He can intervene at any point in time, whenever He chooses, for He is sovereign - however, most of the time He chooses not to, until His people fulfil their role in this supernatural partnership.

... a verse which reminds us of the enormous difference between speaking words into the air and really praying and relating intimately to a living, personal God.

So much from one small verse – sixteen chapters already and several more to come! Now we come to the topic we all want to talk about even less than pride – and that's sin. Given that sin is referred to, in one form or another, well over 1,000 times in the Bible, devoting some time to exploring the reality of sin and our responsibility in dealing with sin is very important.

Given this chapter's title, we must now ask, why is sin a problem? Firstly, it's a problem because sin is bad and so sin is always a problem, and we will look at some reasons for that in the next chapter. However, the other reason sin is a problem for us today is that as New Covenant believers, born in the shadow of the cross, living through the reality of the New Testament, we often struggle with the place and effect of sin in terms of our relationship with God.

This problem is huge because when we have an incorrect view of sin and its impact, we end up making wrong judgements about ourselves, others and God and that leads us into major trouble. So, I plan to spend this entire chapter dealing with this problem before we explore the issue further.

As I have often said, whether we like it or not, our thoughts run our lives and what we think about God, ourselves, others and life in general, will to a large extent determine how we live. The Bible says we are to be "*… transformed by the renewing of our mind*" (Romans 12:2) and that means we have to think. That is hard for some of us, not because we are not intelligent, but because we have not been expected to think all that much in the church for a very long time.

Our culture contributes to this mental laziness in a substantial way. We are bombarded daily with this insidious mindset which says, *"If it feels good it must be right … and if it feels bad it must be wrong."* This is not only in our pagan culture; it is also running rampant in the church. The Pentecostal revival in the early part of last century and the charismatic renewal fifty years ago certainly brought fresh air to the shrinking orthodox church.

People began to experience the reality of God in their lives. A lifeless, fruitless, intellectual understanding of a distant God was transformed in millions of people as they experienced an alive, vibrant, present God, Who touched their very soul and released them from the prison of empty words which they had endured for so long. These movements were controversial; they were attacked and scorned by many, especially those in leadership who felt threatened.

These movements certainly had many human abuses and some demonic distortions, but there is no question that they embodied a move of the Holy Spirit which continues today right across the church in almost every denomination.

However, we humans are renowned for going too far one way or the other! Balance has not been our strong point. Extremes are common. So, in our desire for a real encounter with a living God; one that touches our Spirit and our soul; a relationship which we not only understand with our minds but experience in our soul and our bodies; many have been guilty of parking their brains and embracing the mindset of our hedonistic, experiential, instant-gratification culture.

We've been given the Bible – a collection of ancient writings, inspired by the Holy Spirit, which we claim to be the final authority in this human realm for all matters of faith and practice, and yet this book requires mental *and* spiritual energy to interpret and understand.

It's not enough to give a new believer a Bible and tell them to go and read it and let the Holy Spirit teach them all they need to know. From time to time, there may be no choice and God is certainly able to do so much with very little resources. However, in our day and culture, we are without excuse for not learning how to use the Bible properly.

There is no question that the Holy Spirit is our Teacher, but how does He teach us? Some would say He speaks truth into our spirit, and we just 'know' it because we 'feel' it and 'experience' it. I don't have a major problem with that, for that is what the Spirit has done for me many thousands of times. However, many believe that this is <u>all</u> that we need, and they are wrong.

One of the other ways the Holy Spirit teaches us from the Bible is to show us how to read it properly, understanding how dozens of documents written by fallible human beings over thousands of years from totally different cultural perspectives could come together in one compilation like this and actually make sense and inform our lives.

We need to learn to *interpret* the Bible and *discern* the life-changing eternal Word of God within the pages of Scripture. The Bible is not the literal words of God – we all know that. They are the words of men, compiled by men, translated by men, and then interpreted and taught by men and women! So, we need to remember that, and not expect the Bible to do what it was never intended to do.

Now that whole process was and is under the oversight and direction of the Holy Spirit, there's no question about that, but the Bible is still a complicated collection of documents which requires us to exercise our minds when reading it, interpreting it, and applying it to our lives. So much error and thousands of controversies, disputes and divisions have emerged in the church over the years because people handle the Bible poorly.

Some are guilty of intellectualising the whole thing and without any guidance from the Holy Spirit, they make the Bible say all sorts of things it was never meant to say. Others, however, don't think enough and shamelessly handle the Scriptures as they lift quotes out of context here, there, and everywhere to justify their own particular theological perspective and experience.

Which brings us to the problem before us today: the problem of sin. Our understanding of sin is one of the many areas in which we have seen great divergence of opinion and I want to suggest to you that the controversy, conflict, and confusion in this area is unacceptable and entirely avoidable. If we would just read the Bible properly and learn to interpret Scripture through Scripture before we interpret Scripture though our personal experience, then this confusion about sin would never arise.

Our experience is valid and important - it should not be ignored. The convictions we feel in our heart and the emotions and feelings which accompany them are not to be judged too harshly … but they are to be judged nonetheless, for we are a fallible, fallen people who get it wrong a lot of the time. Our emotions and feelings can (and often do) lie to us and they can also be influenced by the powers of darkness.

That is why the first 'window' through which we should view the Bible is always the Bible itself. By that I mean this. There is a progressive revelation of God and His dealings with mankind running from Genesis through to Revelation and we are meant to have a grasp of the *whole* picture before trying to interpret *parts* of the picture.

If you have been a student of the Bible for a while, you will know that you should not lift any passage you like out of the middle of the Old Testament, written before the coming of Christ, and apply it directly to your experience today, this side of the cross.

There are lots of verses which are universally applicable - many of the Psalms and other passages which speak of the nature of God, apply equally now as when they were written. But there are just as many which do not fit directly into today's context and were never meant to be lifted from their original context.

If you see the Bible unfolding like a journey through time with God revealing more and more of His character and nature and His purpose and plan in redeeming mankind ... then you will realise that some of the commentary on that journey is general observation about God and man and it applies to every leg of that journey. However much of it is about the circumstances at one particular point in that journey and we need to make sure we leave it there and don't lift it out of its context because much of the reality today is very different, thanks to the finished work of Jesus Christ.

It is still valuable information. God still inspired its recording and writing so we can see the big picture. But He never intended for us to put ourselves back into a situation which is locked in time and another culture thousands of years ago.

Most Christians I know, have some measure of understanding about the need to interpret Scripture carefully and use it wisely. But how many know how to do that are they following that principle all the time?

This is a wild statement, I know, but I am going to stick my neck out and say that the majority of believers today do not do this very well and that includes some famous ones who write best-sellers and lead large churches! The saddest thing about all this is that this is totally avoidable. Treating the Bible with respect and learning to interpret it properly is not a difficult task. However, it does require commitment and diligence. In an age of 'instant' everything and 'quick fixes,' this is an area in which we fail because we are a lazy people, and we will not work hard for something if we can get a facsimile of it for much less effort.

That is why so many Christians have a weak Biblical foundation to their faith. They get away with that most days. In fact, some manage to go through their whole life like that. But when someone challenges their beliefs and their concept of God, from inside or outside the Church, many of them stumble and fall to explain *why* they believe what they do.

What then can say about sin? How do we interpret the Bible when it comes to sin in our lives? Well, a good place to start might be 2 Chronicles 7:14 - the very verse we are studying so passionately in this series. This verse clearly states that if the people of God turn from their sin (wicked ways) then God will hear from heaven, forgive their sin and this will have a radical flow-on effect across the entire land.

By inference then, this verse seems to say that if we do *not* turn from our sin, God will *not* hear us, He will *not* forgive us and He will *not* heal our land. Is that right? Is this verse actually saying that God hearing us and forgiving us is conditional upon us humbling ourselves, seeking His face and turning from our sin? Let me give you another one while you are still thinking …

Psalm 66:18 clearly states that if I regard wickedness or iniquity (sin) in my heart, God will not hear me. The premise is that sin separates us from God, and He will not hear our prayer if we have sin in our heart. That is the clear inference of this verse and that is how it's taught in many pulpits right across the world to this very day. But what do you think?

Let's try another one, shall we? There really are many – but I am selecting only a few:

Isaiah 59:1-2 makes it even clearer when it says: *"Surely the arm of the LORD is not too short to save, nor his ear too dull to hear. But your iniquities have separated you from your God; your sins have hidden his face from you, so that he will not hear."*

So, what do you think? *"If my people, who are called by my name, will humble themselves and pray and seek my face and turn from their wicked ways, then will I hear from heaven and (**then I**) will forgive their sin and heal their land."*

Is that what it really means? In its original context: absolutely. This is exactly what it means. So too with the other two passages above and dozens of others. In our fallen, unredeemed state, sin effectively (not theologically) separates us from God. A holy God cannot look upon unatoned sin without judging it. His wrath burns against all unrighteousness.

So, rather than destroy the objects of His deep love, God would effectively turn His back on them until that sin was atoned for through sacrifice. If sin has not been atoned for, it remains a barrier … an impenetrable wall between us and God. That is the reality of life in the Old Testament. That is the truth under which mankind lived under the Old Covenant. Then Jesus came, and absolutely everything changed. The writer of Hebrews explains that change better than anyone.

> *"Day after day every priest stands and performs his religious duties; again and again he offers the same sacrifices, which can never take away sins. But when this priest had offered for all time one sacrifice for sins, he sat down at the right hand of God, and since that time he waits for his enemies to be made his footstool.*
>
> *For by one sacrifice, he has made perfect forever those who are being made holy. The Holy Spirit also testifies to us about this. First, he says: "This is the covenant I will make with them after that time, says the Lord. I will put my laws in their hearts, and I will write them on their minds."*

Then he adds: "Their sins and lawless acts I will remember no more." And where these have been forgiven, sacrifice for sin is no longer necessary." Therefore, brothers and sisters, since we have confidence to enter the Most Holy Place by the blood of Jesus, by a new and living way opened for us through the curtain, that is, his body, and since we have a great priest over the house of God, let us draw near to God with a sincere heart and with the full assurance that faith brings, having our hearts sprinkled to cleanse us from a guilty conscience and having our bodies washed with pure water. Let us hold unswervingly to the hope we profess, for he who promised is faithful." (Hebrews 10:11-23)

This is the good news! This is the gospel! This is what it's all about. This is the wonder, glory and mystery of this incredible salvation which is ours free in Christ! That impenetrable barrier between us and God which would not even allow Him to hear us or forgive us, was smashed once and for all by Jesus when He lived a perfect life for us; paid the price of our sin on the cross (which is what we call 'atonement'); and then conquered sin, death and Satan forever when He rose victorious from the grave. If you have any doubt that Jesus has dealt with the barrier that sin caused, let me read just a few of the many New Testament passages which remind us of this great salvation.

"Praise be to the God and Father of our Lord Jesus Christ, who has blessed us in the heavenly realms with every spiritual blessing in Christ. For he chose us in him before the creation of the world to be holy and blameless in his sight. In love he predestined us for adoption to sonship through Jesus Christ, in accordance with his pleasure and will - to the praise of his glorious grace, which he has freely given us in the One he loves.

In him we have redemption through his blood, the forgiveness of sins, in accordance with the riches of God's grace that he lavished on us. With all wisdom and understanding, he made known to us the mystery of his will according to his good pleasure, which he purposed in Christ, to be put into effect when the times reach their fulfillment -to bring unity to all things in heaven and on earth under Christ.

In him we were also chosen, having been predestined according to the plan of him who works out everything in conformity with the purpose of his will, in order that we, who were the first to put our hope in Christ, might be for the praise of his glory.

And you also were included in Christ when you heard the message of truth, the gospel of your salvation. When you believed, you were marked in him with a seal, the promised Holy Spirit, who is a deposit guaranteeing our inheritance until the redemption of those who are God's possession - to the praise of his glory." (Ephesians 1:3-14)

Wow! What a passage. What an incredible promise! What a mighty and gracious God we serve.

"For this reason, since the day we heard about you, we have not stopped praying for you. We continually ask God to fill you with the knowledge of his will through all the wisdom and understanding that the Spirit gives, so that you may live a life worthy of the Lord and please him in every way: bearing fruit in every good work, growing in the knowledge of God, being strengthened with all power according to his glorious might so that you may have great endurance and patience, and giving joyful thanks to the Father, who has qualified you to share in the inheritance of his holy people in the kingdom of light.

For he has rescued us from the dominion of darkness and brought us into the kingdom of the Son he loves, in whom we have redemption, the forgiveness of sins." (Colossians 1:9-14)

Redemption and forgiveness are a free gift. We do not earn them with our confession or repentance. So, you see, we need to view 2 Chronicles 7:14 and other references through the window of the New Covenant.

Does that mean this part of the verse we are looking at here has no meaning for us? Are we supposed to just ignore this bit because our sin has been atoned for? No - not at all. It still has meaning, and I will unpack that further in the next chapter.

We just need to understand that its original meaning and context does not apply to our journey with God now, this side of the cross, as New Covenant believers upon whom God has lavished grace, mercy and forgiveness and redemption.

Sin is still sin and it's as ugly and destructive today as it ever was. Repentance is still a precious gift and an essential need for New Covenant believers, and we will see why in more detail later. I just need to establish right here and now, before we look at the ongoing problem of sin, that sin no longer separates us from God in the way it may have in the past. Jesus fixed all that – once and for all time. You no longer have to worry if God is listening to your prayers or not because of sin in your life. If you stand in Christ as a believer, then God is listening to all your prayers … no matter how much sin is in your life.

As I will explain later, sin may have a huge impact on your ability to hear from God, so from your perspective, sin can be a real problem, but not from God's perspective. He remembers our sins no more. The slate is clean. Praise the Lord!

So, does that mean that our sin, no matter how bad it gets, can never sever our eternal relationship with God when we are in Christ; when we are a New Covenant, born-again believer? If God is the one Who saves us, does that mean we cannot ever be 'unsaved' again? Well, there are thousands of preachers all over the world who would never be stupid enough to answer such a question in public or even in private for some of them – they certainly would not put it in writing! I'm not sure why this is the case because the answer is simple. The answer is unequivocally, absolutely, positively YES! That is exactly what it means. Your name is written in the Lamb's book of life and no one, not God, not Satan and not even you, can rub it out.

But you may think, what about that very difficult passage in Hebrews 6 which says it is impossible for someone who once tasted the fruit of salvation, to ever come to repentance again if they fall away? Where does that fit? Good question. Some of the most brilliant theologians in the world have tried to work that one out.

What do you do with Matthew 6:14-15 where it says if we forgive others, God will forgive us and we do not forgive, God will not forgive us. If forgiveness is part of salvation; if we are forgiven for all sins, past present and future, what on earth does that mean?

I could go on and quote a few more difficult statements in the New Testament, written this side of cross, written in the context of the New Covenant, which seem to contradict those very bold statements I made earlier. That's why it's so important that we allow the Holy Spirit to teach us how to read and interpret the Bible properly.

Let me tell you that these difficult passages are not a problem for me anymore. I learned a long time ago that you need to pick the right window through which you interpret the Bible. In other words, you need to start at the right place before viewing or seeking to understand these difficult passages. You need to stand on solid ground and look through the largest window possible: that is, established, irrefutable, foundational, Biblical truth.

In this case, we have hundreds of passages in the New Testament which affirm our position in Christ. Dozens which deal very clearly with the issue of atonement for sin and our forgiveness being part of the gift of salvation and not dependent upon our confession or repentance. That is the bedrock upon which you must stand. That is the window of clear, unambiguous truth through which you look to interpret the isolated texts which are not widely supported or explained by other Scriptures.

Sometimes we are able to understand the intent of a difficult passage in the context of the rest of Scripture this way. At other times, the passage remains a mystery and we simply cannot understand it. Perhaps it was translated wrong. Perhaps the writer, in trying to make a point went a little far, like all preachers and writers do at times, and left us with a statement which is now open to misinterpretation. Whatever the reason, it remains a mystery and we just leave it alone and stand firm on that which is clearly understood and supported by all of Scripture.

So let me wrap this chapter up by stating that the problem of sin first and foremost is a problem of understanding what the Bible says about the context and nature of sin now, in our lives as Christians. We cannot allow a loose handling of Scripture, or an ignorance of Old Covenant and New Covenant differences; or a few problem texts to push us out of the mainstream of Biblical truth into a backwater of speculation and error.

As born-again believers, disciples of the Lord Jesus Christ, our sin has been atoned for, once and for all by the blood of Jesus Christ. Our eternal destiny is secure. Our ticket to heaven has been signed by the Father, with the blood of Jesus and that ticket to eternity is guaranteed by the Holy Spirit within us.

If you have ever worried that sin can one day rob you of your ticket to heaven, then your worries can end right now. It won't happen! I am literally staking my life on that truth.

If you allow sin to run away in your life, you will be miserable. You will hurt yourself and others. You will grieve God. You will hinder the work of God. But your eternal destination is secure - just as it was for the brother to whom the Apostle Paul was referring in 1 Corinthians 5:5 when he instructed the leaders to, *"hand this man over to Satan, so that his sinful nature may be destroyed, and his spirit saved on the day of the Lord."*

This brother had allowed sin to run rampant in his life and in these very confronting words of Paul, he makes it clear that this man's soul will be saved on the day of the Lord. We will share heaven with this brother because of the blood of Jesus and the grace of God - not because of his personal performance in this life, which clearly was not good.

So, if you are feeling a little bit better about your sin now; if you are feeling a little more relaxed in the knowledge that you cannot sin your way out of the grace of God, that's good. That's very good, because that is the truth. That is bedrock truth, and we cannot deal with the presence of sin in our lives properly unless that bedrock is firmly established first and never compromised.

In the next chapter I will come from the other side of this and tell you why you must deal with sin ruthlessly; why sin is so evil and insidious and destructive and why I believe God is calling us all to repentance more than at any time in the church's history.

It won't undo anything I have just said, but it will give you the rest of the picture about sin – which we need to know just as clearly. Once we have our eternal salvation squared away, then we can deal with this problem of sin with the right frame of mind, without fear, but with a ruthless honesty and integrity. That's what we'll do next if you decide to keep reading!

If you've struggled with anything you have read in this chapter, please stop here and read it again carefully and prayerfully and talk to God about it. If you're still struggling with the issue of sin and forgiveness and grace, then perhaps my first book, *Amazing Grace,* will help you reconnect with a fuller explanation of God's grace and forgiveness, the foundation of the Gospel and the foundation of all that I have been teaching for decades now.

CHAPTER EIGHTEEN
The Problem of Sin (2)

In the previous chapter, I reinforced the truth that the penalty, the power, and the punishment of sin has been taken from us through the life, death and resurrection of Jesus Christ. That impenetrable barrier between us and God, was smashed once and for all by Jesus when He lived a perfect life for us, atoned for all sin on the cross and then conquered sin, death and Satan forever when He rose victorious from the grave. That is the truth. That is grace. That is the Gospel. That is the good news of Jesus Christ which we are called upon to preach to the world.

Before we looked at the ongoing problem of sin, I needed to establish for some readers, and re-establish for others, that sin no longer separates us from God. Jesus fixed that – once and for all time. You no longer have to worry if God is listening to your prayers because of sin in your life. If you stand in Christ as a believer, then God is listening to all your prayers, in spite of the sin in your life. Yes, this grace in which we stand is THAT radical. We are truly THAT free in Christ.

Now comes the question which Paul faced, and every preacher who has ever made grace as free as God has made it will face: If we are under grace and not under law; if our sin has been atoned for, past, present and future; does that therefore mean that we should not be concerned about sin in our lives anymore?

The answer is, absolutely not! Sin is still just as destructive and evil as it ever was. Sin hurts people. Sin kills people. Sin destroys relationships. Sin distorts truth. Sin projects a false picture of God and leads people away from Him not towards Him. Sin destroys families and church fellowships every day. Sin can also have an impact on our 'experience' of God and our experience of the many blessings He given us in Christ. I will elaborate on all that more in the next chapter, but I want to give you yet another passage which reinforces this foundational understanding of grace, salvation, and forgiveness of sin.

"See to it that no one takes you captive through hollow and deceptive philosophy, which depends on human tradition and the basic principles of this world rather than on Christ. For in Christ all the fullness of the Deity lives in bodily form, and you have been given fullness in Christ, who is the head over every power and authority. In him you were also circumcised, in the putting off of the sinful nature, not with a circumcision done by the hands of men but with the circumcision done by Christ, having been buried with him in baptism and raised with him through your faith in the power of God, who raised him from the dead.

When you were dead in your sins and in the uncircumcision of your sinful nature, God made you alive with Christ. He forgave us all our sins, having cancelled the written code, with its regulations, that was against us and that stood opposed to us; he took it away, nailing it to the cross. And having disarmed the powers and authorities, he made a public spectacle of them, triumphing over them by the cross."(Colossians 2:8-15)

I could write a whole book on this incredible passage (I think I already did!) but let just me just highlight some very powerful and very clear statements of truth here.

"… you have been given fullness in Christ …"

Notice this is past tense. In other words, this has happened. In the package marked 'Salvation' we were given fullness in Christ, which includes all kinds of wonderful goodies like forgiveness, holiness, righteousness, eternal life, abundant life, faith, spiritual gifts … to name just a few!

Now, whether we experience the reality of all those things or not is another issue entirely. Whether we appropriate, apply, use, walk in or exhibit the fruit of that fullness in Christ is always up to us. More about that later. Just understand one thing: all of this has been given to you already, in Christ, as part of the grace and salvation God has lavished upon you as His child.

"When you were dead in your sins … God made you alive with Christ."

Let me ask you a question: can a dead person do anything, other than smell and attract blowflies? No! Dead people are dead. They are totally incapable of doing anything expect rotting away. They are worthless to everyone except the worms! So, it's no accident that the Bible uses the term 'dead' to describe our true spiritual condition prior to receiving salvation.

We need to understand that we were totally and utterly devoid of the ability to desire God or respond to God in any way, shape, or form. We were dead in our sinful, rebellious state. We were born dead: that is, we were all born spiritually bankrupt, and we needed a saviour. We needed someone outside of ourselves to step into our grave and breathe life into our decaying spirits and give us the desire to turn to God.

Well, guess what? God did just that ! Hallelujah! *God made us alive with Christ.* This is the gospel, and you should be leaping with overwhelming joy right about now! God raised us from our spiritual death. But He did more than just wake us up, He dealt with the enemy which killed us in the first place: sin.

"…He forgave us all our sins …"

Fascinating grammar here. The word translated 'forgave' is past tense and the word translated 'all' is present continuous tense. That means that the forgiveness which is given for those sins I commit today (and tomorrow) is all mine <u>before</u> those sins are committed. It is guaranteed – it comes in that glorious package called 'Salvation.' Now I am not hanging that truth just on this one verse. That is stated in many places in the New Testament.

"But what about confession and repentance?" you might ask. An excellent question, which I intend answering in another chapter. It's an easy one to deal with - much clearer than most people think. Just don't let questions like that rob you of the truth of what I have written thus far. He forgave us ALL our sins: past, present and future.

"…having cancelled the written code, with its regulations, that was against us and that stood opposed to us …"

This is referring to the old covenant law of God, that law which defined our sin. Without the Law, there is no definition of sin. The law is what determines right from wrong. So, what is Paul saying here? The law of God has been cancelled? How could that be? Easy, the law was finally fulfilled completely by a human being on behalf of all mankind in Jesus. Jesus obeyed the law of God completely and He did so on our behalf, thereby rendering the old covenant law obsolete, replacing it with a whole new covenant. Just in case you were in doubt as to what "cancelled" means, Paul makes it even clearer:

"... he took it away, nailing it to the cross ..."

The crucifixion of Jesus was, symbolically speaking, the place where the law of God was executed for all time – not because it was bad – but because it was fulfilled, once and for all time, by Jesus, for us. Mankind had proven beyond any doubt that we were totally incapable of obeying God's law - we got it wrong over and over again.

So Jesus came and did it for us; He served our sentence of death, then He rose again three days later and ascended to the Father, only to return in the form of the Holy Spirit so that now, in these New Testament, new covenant days in which we live, the life of Jesus Himself, the fulfiller of the law of God, can be imparted to us and lived through us.

"... and having disarmed the powers and authorities ..."

When Jesus died and the law was nailed to the cross, figuratively speaking, the tool which Satan had used to accuse us before God, namely the written code of the law, was taken away. When a Prosecuting Attorney accuses you before a Judge and stands against you in a courtroom, he can only do that because there is a law which defines your action as a crime. If that law was taken away, you could never be successfully prosecuted, not ever! The Attorney may still accuse you before the Judge, but the Judge's response will always be, *"Sorry Mr Prosecutor, there is no basis for this charge."* Sound familiar? It should. That's what is happening to you 24 hours a day before the throne of God.

" …Now have come the salvation and the power and the kingdom of our God, and the authority of his Christ. For the accuser of our brothers, who accuses them before our God, day and night, has been hurled down. (Revelation 12:10)

Satan continues to accuse us. He continually tries to make us pay for our sins before God, even though Jesus has done that for us. According to Colossians 2, Satan has no authority to accuse us because he has been disarmed by Jesus on the cross. But he will still try. He will torture us through our fallen imagination and conscience all the time.

In fact, he is so relentless in this pursuit that He can actually have an effect on us, if we let him. He can never rob us of our salvation in real terms, but he can rob us of the present experience and assurance of our salvation.

If we don't clearly understand what Colossians 2 and the rest of the New Testament clearly affirms about our salvation and the forgiveness which is ours in Christ, once and for all sin, then we will start to feel guilt and shame all over again and we will effectively re-arm the devil and give him back the tools he needs to beat us up again.

He can't beat us out of heaven – our eternal destiny is secure – but some days it sure feels like that's exactly what he's done! Jesus disarmed the powers and authorities. He removed their authority and said *"ALL authority therefore is given to ME."* That doesn't leave much authority for Satan, does it? Not unless we give it back to him. How can we do that? It's simple. We give Satan authority over us by receiving his accusations, by falling away from grace and coming back under the law again. God still doesn't listen to the enemy's accusations, but we do, and that's why so many redeemed children of God continue to battle with guilt and shame. They are not walking in the truth.

When we are not rooted and grounded in truth; when we do not understand everything that the life, death and resurrection of Jesus achieved for us, then Satan can pick us off like sitting ducks and down we go in discouragement, depression and fear.

The other way in which we effectively give Satan authority over us again is through our ongoing sin. Satan inhabits the sin of God's people. We open the door to him by our sin. We "agree with him" in one sense. He finds something within us (sin) which resonates with his character and his agenda and so an unholy 'connection' is formed, and we effectively invite him into our lives along with his ministry of deception, discouragement and despair. We can be substantially free from the enemy's influence and attack if we keep the two doors shut through which he enters most often: ignorance and sin.

I will have more to say on this in future chapters, but let me close this chapter with one of the many passages throughout the New Testament which sums up what God has done for us. Read this a few times and really let this truth bless you.

> *"For we know that since Christ was raised from the dead, he cannot die again; death no longer has mastery over him. The death he died, he died to sin once for all; but the life he lives, he lives to God. In the same way, count yourselves dead to sin but alive to God in Christ Jesus.*
>
> *Therefore, do not let sin reign in your mortal body so that you obey its evil desires. Do not offer the parts of your body to sin, as instruments of wickedness, but rather offer yourselves to God, as those who have been brought from death to life; and offer the parts of your body to him as instruments of righteousness. For sin shall not be your master, because you are not under law, but under grace." (Romans 6:9-14)*

CHAPTER NINETEEN
The Present Reality of Sin

In the last two chapters I addressed the issue of sin from the perspective of our relationship with God, re-establishing and pressing home the truth of the gospel, the good news of Jesus Christ, the message of grace and forgiveness which God spoke to us in these last days through the life, death and resurrection of His Son, our Saviour, the Lord Jesus Christ. Now I want us to look at sin face-to-face, in the here-and-now, cause-and-effect, human realm where we live. However, I first want to remind us, yet again, of the backdrop to this study of sin. We can never be reminded of this too many times - it is a safeguard. So here is the story of creation, sin, law, grace, redemption, and salvation in a nutshell. This is the gospel story.

Once upon a time, we were created by God for His pleasure; to be in close relationship with Him; to walk in the Garden of Intimacy with Him day and night, sharing our heart and life and enjoying this wonderful creation and life in close harmony with our loving Father. We were created with total freedom, which included the freedom to step outside the boundaries set by our Father … therefore, we were free to disobey Him … and we did. He told us lots of things we should do in this freedom and one thing we should not do … and we allowed the enemy of God to lie to us and tempt us and we rebelled and broke the heart of our loving Father.

Sin entered this perfect world and changed everything. Sin will always bring a consequence – then and now. It certainly brought a huge consequence back then. Our sin repelled us from God's presence and drove us out of the Garden of Intimacy. A holy God cannot look upon sin without burning against it in judgement – God's love for us was unaltered; He was not being mean; He was just being Holy; He can be nothing less and holiness cannot co-exist with unholiness any more than light can co-exist with darkness. Put light and darkness together and light will always repel the darkness.

So, the wrath, judgement and holiness of God was then revealed against sin. The law of God was given through Moses to define our sin. The law was not needed before sin entered the world. The sacrificial system was introduced to try and appease God and somehow deal with this barrier which had formed between God and His precious children. All through the Old Testament we see God going to incredible lengths to provide for our sin and warn us and call us back to Himself. Day after day after year after generation, God was calling us to repentance and calling us to return to Him.

The old covenant provided a way for that to happen - but it just didn't work. There was nothing wrong with the old covenant. There was nothing wrong with the law of God and the sacrificial system and everything else God put in place to provide for our sin. What was wrong was us! We were the problem – not the old covenant. We simply could not make the grade. We could not obey the holy law of God.

We kept slipping and falling into sin again and that kept us at arm's length to God and broke His heart, for He was desperate longing to walk with us again in the Garden of Intimacy. The old covenant was not wrong, but it certainly was ineffective.

Our loving God was so committed to us, that He launched the most radical rescue bid in the history of the universe! This rescue mission made Rambo look like a wimp! This was radical. This was incredible. God was going to save the whole world, but not in a way that anyone expected. God Himself took responsibility for *our* problem – the problem of sin. Even though it was *our* fault; even though *we* were the ones who messed up and failed to obey the law of God; even though this was *our* problem - God made it *His* problem - because He was a hundred times more committed to His relationship with us, than we were.

So, the God of this universe; the Creator and Sustainer of all life; stepped out of eternity and into time and space; He left the glory of heaven as a spiritual being and entered a teenager's womb, to be born as a mortal human being, named Jesus.

This God-man, Jesus, was the long awaited Messiah and Saviour Whom the Jews had heard prophecies about for generations. Although wholly God, He set aside His status and power and humbled Himself to become one of us. He submitted to all the limitations of time and space. He had to communicate with the Father, through the Holy Spirit, just like us. He was wholly man – facing all the struggles, limitations, and temptations we all face.

As a man, Jesus was the first human to obey the law of God fully and completely. He fulfilled the law, the Bible says. Whilst doing that, He also gathered some disciples together and taught them about what God was doing and why. He planted truth in their hearts and a seed of life that would last well beyond His time here in the flesh. When that teaching and training was over, He then completed His earthly mission.

Not only did He have to fulfil the law, on our behalf, He also had to pay the price for our rebellion, because the wages of sin is death. So, Jesus died. This innocent man was murdered as a criminal, in accordance with God's will. There was no other way to redeem us.

He then rose from the dead and returned to the right hand of the Father, thereby conquering sin, death and Satan, and completing the mission of saving the lost children of God. In our powerless, hopeless, rebellious, sinful, spiritually dead state - God came to us and breathed life into our spirit! What grace! What mercy! What a mighty and loving God we serve!

Now, as we embrace His free offer of salvation, we are, in spiritual terms, 'united with Him' in His life, in His death and in His resurrection. Which means His perfect obedience becomes our perfect obedience before God. His death becomes our death and His resurrection to new life becomes our resurrection. Jesus came to earth and scored straight A's on the report card of life and then, in the most mysterious, glorious and wonderful exchange in the history of the universe, Jesus put your name and mine on the top of that report card - that perfect performance - and He handed it to the Father and said, *"It is finished."*

That's right - Jesus paid for your ticket to heaven with His life. So now, as we embrace that truth in faith; as we accept the good news – the gospel; our eyes are opened and we see that we have been given forgiveness of sins, past, present and future! We have righteousness and holiness and eternal life and hope and grace and mercy and love and power flowing in us and through us, all because of Jesus Christ.

When we receive the salvation offered to us in Christ, we die to our old life … we die to the law, which we could never obey … and we receive new life - His life. That's why Paul said this:

> *"For through the law I died to the law so that I might live for God. I have been crucified with Christ and I no longer live, but Christ lives in me. The life I live in the body, I live by faith in the Son of God, who loved me and gave himself for me. I do not set aside the grace of God, for if righteousness could be gained through the law, Christ died for nothing!" (Galatians 2:19-21)*

Praise God for His love! Praise God for His amazing grace! Praise God for His wonderful salvation. Once and for all - Jesus has done it. His was the final sacrifice. Holy we stand before His throne because Jesus paid the price! Paul said it very clearly to the Colossians believers:

> *"When you were dead in your sins and in the uncircumcision of your sinful nature, God made you alive with Christ. He forgave us all our sins, having cancelled the written code, with its regulations, that was against us and that stood opposed to us; he took it away, nailing it to the cross. And having disarmed the powers and authorities, he made a public spectacle of them, triumphing over them by the cross." (Colossians 2:13-15)*

The law which defined our sin was fulfilled in Jesus and thereby rendered irrelevant in terms of the judgement of God against us. A new covenant, a new agreement, a new day was ushered in by Jesus. Praise God! So, what then do we say about sin now? We are completely forgiven, cleansed, reconciled, and made holy before God because of Jesus.

Our eternal destiny is secured by God in Christ. Our salvation was secured 2,000 years ago before we even committed our first sin or asked for forgiveness! So, what do we say about sin? Sin is still with us; sin is still very real. We still trip and fall and disobey. We still lie and steal. We still commit the sin of laziness and idleness. We gossip and slander and destroy relationships - and that's just in the church!

Sin is still sin, and sin is still our daily companion. So, is sin still a problem? Given that we are forgiven for all sin, is it something we should still be concerned about? Absolutely! There's no question about it. Read the New Testament; read page after page of exhortations from Jesus and Paul and others to face our sin head-on and deal with it ruthlessly – every day!

We know where we are headed. As we pray that the Kingdom of God will come in power and glory, we know that one day we will not have to struggle with sin in our mortal bodies - but for now, we do. Even Paul, the great Apostle of God; the one who preached grace and forgiveness and freedom from sin more than anyone who ever lived; even Paul had a very human struggle with sin. This is a long passage, but it's really worth studying:

> *"I do not do the good I want to do, but the evil I do not want to do - this I keep on doing. Now if I do what I do not want to do, it is no longer I who do it, but it is sin living in me that does it. So, I find this law at work: Although I want to do good, evil is right there with me. For in my inner being I delight in God's law; but I see another law at work in me, waging war against the law of my mind and making me a prisoner of the law of sin at work within me. What a wretched man I am! Who will rescue me from this body that is subject to death? Thanks be to God, who delivers me through Jesus Christ our Lord!*
>
> *"So then, I myself in my mind am a slave to God's law, but in my sinful nature a slave to the law of sin. Therefore, there is now no condemnation for those who are in Christ Jesus, because through Christ Jesus the law of the Spirit who gives life has set you free from the law of sin and death."*

"For what the law was powerless to do because it was weakened by the flesh, God did by sending his own Son in the likeness of sinful flesh to be a sin offering. And so he condemned sin in the flesh, in order that the righteous requirement of the law might be fully met in us, who do not live according to the flesh but according to the Spirit."

"Those who live according to the flesh have their minds set on what the flesh desires; but those who live in accordance with the Spirit have their minds set on what the Spirit desires. The mind governed by the flesh is death, but the mind governed by the Spirit is life and peace. The mind governed by the flesh is hostile to God; it does not submit to God's law, nor can it do so. Those who are in the realm of the flesh cannot please God."

"You, however, are not in the realm of the flesh but are in the realm of the Spirit, if indeed the Spirit of God lives in you. And if anyone does not have the Spirit of Christ, they do not belong to Christ. But if Christ is in you, then even though your body is subject to death because of sin, the Spirit gives life because of righteousness.

And if the Spirit of him who raised Jesus from the dead is living in you, he who raised Christ from the dead will also give life to your mortal bodies because of[e] his Spirit who lives in you."
(Romans 7:19–8:11)

That's a Bible passage I deliberately read often. It is one of the many texts where Paul paints the big picture for us. In such a masterful way, he shows us the problem of sin and the solution for sin in one concise teaching and in a balanced way which communicates the wonder of our salvation, redemption, and forgiveness, yet deals with the reality of sin in our lives today and what we need to do about it.

As new covenant, born-again believers; as Christians, we have a choice every morning when we wake up; we have a choice every second of every minute of every hour of every day: we can live according to Spirit or to we can live according to the flesh.

In Romans 8:1-4, Paul makes it very clear that we have been set free from the law of sin and death by God in Christ. Paul does what I have attempted to do in the last few chapters, and indeed the last forty years of my teaching, he establishes the truth of our forgiveness and redemption from sin. However, in the following verses he immediately talks about the daily choice that we face to live according to the sinful nature or live according to the Spirit within us.

Paul has clearly identified with all believers who desire to please God and live a life worthy of their calling in Christ. Paul has admitted that he still struggles with sin. Then he tells us why that is the case. We struggle with sin because we *choose* to sin. We struggle with sin because we make the choice to submit to the sinful nature within us rather than the Spirit of God within us. Basically, that means we continue to sin because we *want* to sin.

It's our choice and it's our fault when we sin and we have to face the consequences of sin like grown-ups and not pass the buck to other people, to God or even to Satan. Yes, even Satan! In Jesus' name please understand this … Adam and Eve were the first humans to say, *"The devil made me do it,"* and billions of us have followed in their footsteps! Colossians 2:15 tells us that Jesus disarmed the Devil and took away his authority over us. The New Testament tells us to resist the Devil and he will flee from us. We are told to not give the Devil a foothold, implying that he cannot take a foothold without our permission.

The powers of darkness can come against us in a myriad of ways. The Bible warns us about Satan and how he prowls day and night seeking to devour us - and he will, if we let him - but he can't if we know how to slam the door in his face! Quite simply, Satan 'inhabits' the sins we commit. When we 'open the door' to him by choosing to sin, he needs no encouragement to come in and manifest his evil presence in us and around us. We all need to take responsibility for that and stop talking about being 'under spiritual attack' in a way which implies we had no control over it. We may well be under attack, but we need to ask, *"Did I invite this attack by the choices I made?"* For example:

- We gossip and then cry 'unfair' when relationships crumble around us.
- We stretch the truth and then cry 'unfair' when people stop trusting our word.
- We punish our bodies for years through neglect and then cry 'unfair' when we get sick.
- We spend most of our time, energy and money on earthly pursuits and then cry 'unfair' when those around us who made different choices seem to have a deeper relationship with God.
- We fill our minds with garbage from television, films and the internet and then cry 'unfair' when we discover our moral standards have slipped.
- We make little or no attempt to build relationships in our church and then cry 'unfair' when we feel lonely.
- We treat people poorly and then cry 'unfair' when they distance themselves from us.
- We fail to honour God in the way we live at home and then cry 'unfair' when our children reject the Church later.

The list goes on. Yes, I know that some things happen to us which are outside our control. Tragedies, accidents, and unexpected changes in life's circumstances. Welcome to planet Earth! We all face that, in varying degrees. However, we are still completely responsible for our reaction to those situations. They can make us stronger, or they can destroy us - it's our choice! They can mature us and drive us deeper into God - or they can leave us in a whimpering heap on the floor wondering why God has deserted us. It's totally up to us how we respond to everything life dishes up. Sin is still a problem for you and me because we keep making the wrong choices – it's as simple as that. We need to make the right choices and we need to be reminded of how evil, destructive, and horrible sin still is.

When we choose to submit to the sinful nature within us and not the Spirit of God, we hurt ourselves; we hurt others; we throw mud on the name of Jesus; we cause others to stumble; we inhibit the flow of the gospel; we destroy relationships and churches and cities and nations.

We invite the enemy of God to come and lay the guilt and shame of sin upon us again - that guilt and shame which Jesus took away on the cross, is returned to us tenfold when Satan is given access to our hearts and minds through our sin.

When that happens, we *feel* unforgiven and dirty; we can't hear God's voice like we used to; we feel like God has turned His back on us. Of course, He hasn't, He is right there where He always was, but our choices, our sin, has muddied the waters so we can't see clearly. Our sin has introduced 'static' in the transmissions from God and so even though He hears every word we pray; we find it increasingly difficult to hear from Him or experience His presence. We effectively re-arm the Devil and give him authority over us again through our sin.

We can't control God. We can't control Satan. We can't control those around us. We can't control life's circumstances – things happen when we least expect them. There is only one thing in the universe we can control and that is <u>our choices</u>.

Until we understand that simple, but vitally important truth, and take responsibility for the choices we make and the consequences which follow those choices – we will continue to be sitting ducks for the enemy of God and everyone around us who may want to manipulate us or shoot us down.

We can sit and sulk and say, *"O woe is me, my life is a mess … people are so mean … God has deserted me … Satan is attacking me …I can't do anything to get out of this torment…"*

We can carry on like that our whole life if we so choose, and we may even find a few unhelpful friends who will hold our hand and cry with us and give us sympathy and encourage us in our cesspool of self-inflicted consequences - rather than confront us, in love, with the truth and help us face life like a grown-up.

Your eternal security in Christ is nailed down as a believer; your ticket to heaven is bought and paid for by Jesus; but your poor choices can put you into a living hell in this life.

Sin is a choice, a very bad choice, a choice that has devastating consequences in this life, a choice which can unleash the powers of darkness into your life, your family, your workplace, your church, your city and your nation - but it's a choice nevertheless - it's *your* choice, today and every day.

We have the power to choose good and evil – that was restored to us by Jesus. We just need to choose good. As Paul said, we need to "*… set our minds on what the Spirit of God desires*" and not on what our sinful nature desires, and we need to do that every morning and all through each day. There is not a second that goes by when we are not faced with that choice.

CHAPTER TWENTY
Confession and Repentance

As we continue looking at the problem of sin, I want to address the issue of confession and repentance. These are two theological terms which have been the subject of thousands of sermons and books and yet are they are still misunderstood by so many. The best possible way I can approach this chapter is to first tell you a story. I guess that's why Jesus told stories all the time. Let me do the same. This is not my story, in fact Jesus told it first. This is just my revised version. Let me share it with you as a backdrop to our study of confession and repentance.

As you read this story, I want you to picture the scenes and the characters in your mind. Connect with them in your heart, and the Spirit of God will teach you more in this one story than I could teach you in fifty books.

- - - - - - - - - - -

A tired, hungry, lonely young man stands with an empty bucket in his hands. He watches the pigs eat the slop and quietly licks his fingers. He thinks back to his early days, kicks the dust, and wonders how he ever ended up in this place. He looks around, but he's alone. It's just him and the swine, and now that he has dumped the food for them, they pay him no attention either. As he stands there, the bitter irony of this scene breaks through in one clear moment of despair: *even the pigs are better off than him!*

Raised on his father's farm, as a good Jewish boy, the suggestion that one day he would be feeding pigs - no, it's worse than that: the suggestion that one day he would be envious of what the pigs were eating - well, that would have seemed impossible back then. Bu that was many, many miles ago. That was before he boldly set out on his own; confident that he knew best - eager to experience all of life. He was breaking free! That's how he had thought about it. And indeed, for a while the freedom felt like a wild wind rushing through his hair: it was glorious and exciting.

But when the money ran out, so did his new-found friends and the wind in his hair became a piercing chill deep in his soul. The famine in the land is like a metaphor of his life. Standing there in the feedlot, his heart feels even emptier than his stomach. The growling in his spirit cries out to be fed; he is having hunger pains of the soul. But there's no one around - no one who cares. Love is as distant as the angry echo of an old bitter argument.

He squints his eyes and turns to look back into the west. Deep in his spirit he feels a stirring, just for a moment, like something (or someone) is calling him. Though it seems a lifetime away, he has a fleeting memory of a time when warm hugs were as common as laughter. The feeling is gone as quickly as it comes, as the reality of life crashes in again and he licks the slop off his fingers once more in an attempt to ease the pain in his stomach.

Across the miles and far, far away, a father wipes the corner of his eye as he looks again down a long, empty road. It has become a habit now that he can't seem to break. Every time he walks from the house to the field, he looks down the road and wonders, and hopes, and longs for the day when his love will once again be received and enjoyed by his precious child.

Sometimes the wind creates a dust cloud on the road and just for a moment his heart leaps and he starts to run towards it, but then it blows away. There's a place in his heart that grieves far more than any anger or disappointment he may have once felt. For him, love conquered hurt long ago and he longs for a way to send a 'welcome back' message out around the world so that his lost son may hear it and return to him. Every night the father looks at an empty chair at the table and thinks of a lost treasure.

They are far apart, these two, and yet they are just a heartbeat away. Grace is about to break out and spill its joyful tears on the embrace of reconciliation. The moment is building when love will overcome every obstacle and all distance will be removed. Grace happens when the emptiness of sin, rebellion and self-inflicted consequences are met by the welcome of love, mercy, and forgiveness. Grace is a hospitality of the heart that always overcomes the estrangement of broken relationships.

No matter how far away the child has wandered; no matter how distant and estranged he feels; no matter how hopeless things may seem - the genetic bond cannot be broken - the linking of hearts between father and child - and the memory of home will aways be there. No matter how hurt the father's heart has been; no matter how much he has had to endure; no matter how long he has suffered - it cannot break the memory of his child nor quench his desire to hold him again and lavish grace and love and forgiveness upon him.

In the midst of famine, there remains the memory of home. In the place of feast, there is a welcome for the wayward child. We live our lives between famine and feast – at times feeling so estranged that we wonder how God could possibly even care; other times overwhelmed by the news that, even so, God holds open for us a place of welcome called 'home.'

The prodigal suffers in this famine and has nothing to eat. In fact, he begins to envy the food that the pigs get, and yet in the midst of the famine he remembers a dinner table. It is a table where even the hired help never go hungry. And then it comes again - that conviction; that sense; that inner calling; that stirring in his spirit; somehow, in the midst of his rebellion and sin, he feels drawn to his home; not as a son anymore; Heaven forbid - he is no longer worthy to be called a son. He ponders the idea of going home as just a lowly servant! Anything to stay alive. There is nowhere else to go, and so, he decides to go back and plead with his father to make him one of his servants.

There begins his long, tiring journey home, all the way thinking of the many reasons why his Father would probably not even let him onto his land, much less into his home! But now and then, as he stops to rest his exhausted, malnourished body, something (or someone) feeds his soul as the longing for home grows. As the scenery becomes familiar, the son realises that he is very close to his father's home. Very soon he will no longer wonder about his father's response - he will know for sure. His heart beats faster - he's not sure if it's fear or hope. Perhaps it's both.

The father looks for the 1,000th time down the road - weary of disappointment and weary of love ungiven. But this time the cloud of dust is filled with promise – the wind does not blow this one away - it moves with a familiar pace; it holds a hopeful step. The father's joy sends him running full speed down the road calling behind him: "*My child is back! The one I thought dead is alive. Set the table! Prepare a feast! We must celebrate! For my son was lost and now he is found; he was dead but now he is alive.*"

As the son lifts his weary head from the dusty road, he can see someone running and shouting. His heart leaps into his throat as he anticipates the worst. Can his father's anger still be so strong after all this time? Will he now face the full consequences of his rebellion as the well-deserved wrath of his father is poured out upon him. Should he turn back? Was this a stupid idea? Why would his father even think of letting him work on the farm after what he did to him?

In the midst of this mental anguish and turmoil he looks again at this rare site of his father running towards him. He had never seen him run before. In fact, he had never seen any Jewish elder run - it just wasn't right. Then he noticed his face; his father was not angry at all - he was actually overwhelmed with joy. Tears ran down his face as he ran towards his beloved son with arms outstretched, and to the utter amazement of the son, before he could even open his mouth, he felt the embrace of grace as it completely overwhelmed the shame of sin.

The love of his father enveloped the son in an instant. In utter amazement and total bewilderment, the son knew that those brief longings he had experienced in the foreign land; those little convictions; those little oases in the desert; were in fact the love of his father inside him. A love which had been there all his life; a love so strong that it could not be totally extinguished by his rebellion and sin. In this holy moment, in this sombre, yet exhilarating moment, godly sorrow overwhelmed the son. A sorrow which tore his heart in two. Not a worldly sorrow which is sorry for getting caught out, but a deep Godly sorrow for the pain and hurt he had inflicted on one who loved him so much.

Confession came easy in the environment of grace and love and the son took ownership of his sin. He was forgiven before he confessed - his father's grace and love was overwhelming - but grace and truth came together, and sin was called sin and admitted, and the first fruit of that amazing grace, as always, was repentance. From that day forward, the son was a changed man. His view of himself, His father and life had changed forever because he responded to the call to come home. The grace of his father was not without effect.

- - - - - - - - - - -

I would encourage you to ponder that story in your mind. Maybe even read it a few more times over the coming days. It's the story of your life. It's not just a story of conversion – not just a story about coming to God once when we accepted His free gift of salvation. It's a story which reminds us of our relationship with the Father - every day - and I believe it's a story which tells us a lot about sin, confession and repentance.

So, what is confession? Confession means 'to say the same thing about' something. To 'agree.' To speak the truth. To confess our sins literally means that we agree with God and call sin what it is. It means we speak the truth about sin in our own lives. We don't hide behind other terms. When we are gossiping, we don't say we are sharing our concerns so we may pray for the person! When we lie, we call it a lie and we don't try and explain it away.

The Bible says that we should confess our sins to one another that we may be healed. What does that mean? It means we get stuff which is in the dark and bring it into the light. Satan loves it when we try to hide our sins. He works in secret, in the shadows, in the hidden, dark places. When we bring something into the open – into the light – it loses so much of its power over us.

The old saying: *Confession is good for the soul* is true if it's done in the right way with a sincere motive. But genuine confession is the fruit of something else. In our story of the prodigal son, there was something which triggered or made that confession easy. Clearly it was the love and grace of the Father.

The love, grace, mercy and forgiveness of the Father brought the son to a place where confession was easy – it was essential – it was inevitable. When faced with the glory of love, forgiveness, and grace, you cannot continue to hide your sin. It is in that environment of grace that confession is released. That leads us to the most quoted verse in the New Testament about confession and sin ... and, I believe, the one of the most misunderstood.

> *"If we confess our sins, God is faithful and just to forgive us and cleanse us from all unrighteousness." (1 John 1:9)*

Because of the limitations of our English translations, we find that the inference in this verse and a few others in the New Testament, lead some of us to conclude that the forgiveness of God is conditional upon our confession. That if we do not confess our sins, He will not forgive them. There are a couple of other verses which seem to indicate that our forgiveness from God is conditional upon our forgiveness of others or some other action on our part.

How do we interpret these verses against the many others you read in the last few chapters of this book which clearly state that forgiveness of sins comes as part of the package of salvation and is not conditional upon anything we do ... other than believe and receive? That's a good question. That is why I stressed a few chapters ago that we need to learn to interpret the Bible properly and look through the right 'windows' when reading some texts.

Getting back to 1 John 1:9, I believe an equally valid translation of the Greek, which is totally consistent with the fuller revelation of the whole New Testament, would read something like this:

> *"God is faithful and just and has forgiven us our sins, so if we confess our sin, we will experience the fruit of that forgiveness and cleansing from all unrighteousness."*

In other words, the reality of our forgiveness is unconditional. God has done it. Jesus paid the price and forgiveness is ours. Sin no longer separates us from the love of God.

However, the experience and fruit of that forgiveness in this life is still impacted by our actions. That is the only way we can interpret this and other verses in the New Testament which imply that if we don't do certain things, this forgiveness is not ours. In terms of our experience and what appears to be real – that is true. In terms of what God has already done and secured for us – that is a different story.

Just think about our story again of the prodigal returning home to his father. Was the grace, love and forgiveness of the father triggered in any way by the confession of the son? No! Dear old dad was running and shouting and crying before the son said a word! He had embraced, accepted, and kissed the son <u>before</u> any confession came. So, was the son's confession necessary? Yes! Absolutely. It was necessary for <u>him</u>.

The son would not have been able to enjoy the fullness of his father's love and grace unless he spoke the truth and brought his sin into the light. In an environment of love and kindness and grace, that confession was so much easier. That's why the Bible says in Romans 2:4 that it's God's *kindness* that leads us to repentance, and repentance is always preceded by confession.

Confession is so important, and so neglected, I'm sorry to say. As the new covenant and God's grace takes hold of us and we bask in the love and forgiveness of God and glory in His amazing grace, there are many who believe that there is a huge danger, that we will forget about sin and confession. I don't happen to be one of those people.

I believe in the power of God's amazing grace. I believe in the power of His love, and I know this from personal experience and from the experience of thousands of people over the years in whom I have observed this: when we truly connect with the love and grace of God, confession of sin will automatically flow. If it doesn't, then we have not encountered God's grace. When we truly encounter the unbridled grace of God, unconfessed sin cannot remain hidden, it is guaranteed. Genuine grace is always accompanied by truth – and especially truth about sin.

John 1:14 says that Jesus was full of grace and truth and a few verses later it says that the law came through Moses, but grace and truth came through Jesus Christ. What does that mean? Well, if you've been around my teaching any length of time, you should know what it means to say that grace comes through Jesus Christ. But what about truth? These two are to be kept in balance, like flip sides to the same coin, they are inseparable.

Grace, forgiveness, love, mercy, and the free gift of eternal life all came to us in Jesus, hallelujah! But so did truth. The implications of that require another book, but for our purposes here, we need to understand that truth means we continue to identify sin as sin, and we bring it into the light immediately. Forgiven or not, sin is still sin and unless we confess it and bring it out of the shadows and allow the love and grace of God to have its effect in this earthly kingdom as it has already had its effect in the kingdom of God then we will not be manifesting the fullness of Christ.

If our calling is to be Christlike, or more specifically, if we are called to submit to the life of Christ within us, so it's no longer we who live but Christ who lives within us, then we too, will be full of grace and truth. We need to allow the grace of God to overwhelm us as we join the prodigal in confessing our sin – quickly, sincerely and as often as we need to - so that all the cleansing, restoring effect of God's grace and forgiveness in Christ, becomes our lived experience.

What about repentance then? The way that term is used by many today, one might ask what the difference is between confession and repentance. I have heard many people stand before a group of believers and repent this sin or that sin. Many people confess their sins but call it repentance. Confession can happen in an instant, with a sentence or two spoken and it's all over. Whereas repentance is the fruit which is meant to follow confession.

Many definitions of repentance have been suggested over the years and they all say something similar. To repent is to change your mind with the intent to change your actions. Therefore, repentance is a process, and it follows confession.

The Holy Spirit convicts us of our sin and our need for change. That conviction results in our confession – where we agree with the Spirit of God and admit that we are off the mark. Repentance (a change of mind, heart, attitude, and actions) is then supposed to follow that confession. Unfortunately, that is not always what happens for many of us.

It is entirely possible for us to stop at that point in the process, for that is the easy part. As hard as it might seem at times to get to the point of confessing a sin, the tough stuff is repentance: where we have to change our thinking and change our direction so that this sin is not a problem in the future. God is there to help us and empower us to change, but the choice is still ours and until we make that choice, true repentance will elude us.

The Apostle Paul preached grace more than anyone I know, and yet the balance of grace and truth was clear in his teaching and his life. He continued to battle with sin in his own life and he dealt with it ruthlessly - not because his salvation depended upon it - he knew he was saved regardless of his ongoing confession or repentance. Paul dealt ruthlessly with sin because he knew that it was the open door to the enemy of God, Satan, to frustrate his life and ministry and rob him of the effectiveness he so earnestly desired as he fulfilled his calling. He wanted to walk in a manner that was worthy of the calling he had in Christ.

Paul knew that God's amazing grace and forgiveness was total and complete; his spiritual bank account was full because of what Jesus secured for him by His life, death and resurrection. But Paul also knew that confession and repentance were his responsibility if he was going to cash any spiritual cheques on that account and see the fruit of that forgiveness. If grace was to ever have its effect, then he had to make sure confession and repentance were a very real part of his daily life.

But even repentance is a gift from God. Yes, we most certainly have a responsibility in that we need to make the choice to change, but even that is a gift, empowered by God.

"God exalted (Christ) to his own right hand as Prince and Saviour that he might give repentance and forgiveness of sins ..." (Acts 5:31)

2 Timothy 2:25 and Acts 11:18 both talk about God *"granting us repentance"* and leading us to the truth. Repentance cannot happen without confession. Until we agree with the Holy Spirit and call sin what it is, then true repentance cannot occur. But confession will not occur without the conviction of the Holy Spirit, and I believe that the primary way the Spirit of God brings genuine conviction which leads us to confession and repentance is by overwhelming us with the love of God. He never does it by accusing us.

There are many Christians in the world right now who are crushed under the weight of accusation from the enemy, and they mistakenly think that is the conviction of the Spirit.

In John 5:45 Jesus clearly told the Pharisees, *"... do not think I will accuse you before the Father. Your accuser is Moses, on whom your hopes are set."*

The law accuses; Satan accuses us by trying to apply the law against us. Whereas God always convicts us by overwhelming us with His love and grace.

I appreciate that what I have written in this chapter may not be popular in many parts of the church and even you might struggle with it. But I really do believe in God's amazing grace and the transforming power of His love! I will therefore go to my grave proclaiming His grace in harmony with truth.

This is what I preached before I saw the fruit of it - but now I have seen the power of that grace. When I started preaching about God's love and grace in a consistent, 'unplugged' manner many years ago, I had a barrage of criticism as people accused me of being soft on sin and said that I needed to 'balance' grace with a bit of law. I find that to be a fascinating concept – mixing grace and law. That's like trying to find a dry spot on the bottom of a swimming pool – it can't happen.

When I started preaching God's grace in a concentrated way many years ago, I believed that God's grace would have its effect and not only lift the guilt and shame and pharisaic expectation off people's shoulders, but it would lead people to repentance faster than any preaching of law or judgement … and I was right. Within a couple of months of me focussing on the grace of God, people started making appointments to speak with me and to my amazement, they started confessing all this stuff which they had locked away and hidden for years! This was truly amazing. Some of these people were leaders in the church at the time. Some of them had carried stuff for a decade or more and never found an environment of grace, acceptance, and love in which they could confess it. God finally healed wounds and released people from the torment of unconfessed sin, when they realised that He was not going to judge them, and nor was I.

When they understood that forgiveness was already theirs, long before they confessed that sin, in fact, long before they even committed that sin; when that truth came to light in their minds and hearts, they couldn't wait to get that stuff out and see the transforming power of God's grace at work. This is the truth of the gospel. This is the good news. This is our God at work.

Can you see your Father running? Can you hear Him shouting and rejoicing as you 'come home'? Let Him embrace you and kiss you and love you back to life. Let His forgiveness and grace and mercy and unconditional love have its effect in you as you confess your sins to Him and to others. Let His gift of repentance be birthed in you as you see His transforming power at work.

Sin is a huge problem in the church today. We deny it, we ignore it, we refuse to call it what it is, and I believe the primary reason that's the case is because we are yet to understand the harmony of grace and truth and so we continue to see two extremes at work every day. There are Christians all over world who are allowing the accusations of the enemy to beat them up and dump shame and guilt and despair upon them which paralyses them and robs them of the power of God. They know some truth, but they know very little grace.

Then there are those who are on the opposite end of the spectrum who refuse to examine their attitudes and actions and allow the Spirit of God to convict them of their sin. They know some grace, but they know very little truth. The law came through Moses, but *grace and truth* came though Jesus.

Come Holy Spirit ... be our Guide ... be our Teacher ... show us the way. May we submit to the life of Jesus more in us each day as grace and truth emerge in everything we think, everything we say, everything we do and everything we pray. Amen

CHAPTER TWENTY-ONE
God Will Heal our Land

"If my people, who are called by my name, will humble themselves and pray and seek my face and turn from their wicked ways, then I will hear from heaven, and I will forgive their sin and will heal their land."(2 Chronicles 7:14)

We come now to the final chapter in this book. I have spent a lot of time exploring the truths in this one verse in 2 Chronicles 7:14 and the many side-roads which flow from it. We've also used this verse as a springboard to study a number of important issues including humility, pride, prayer, faith, the sovereignty of God, intimacy with God, sin, confession, repentance and of course, grace - to mention just a few!

We've explored so many foundational principles of the Christian life in this book. It has been a challenging journey and one in which we've been encouraged to see that we are called into a partnership with our God – a partnership in which we have a responsibility and a significant part to play.

Throughout this teaching I've always attempted to re-interpret or apply this verse in a new covenant, New Testament context so as to avoid the common error perpetrated by many who try to apply Old Testament, Old-Covenant Scriptures directly to our lives today, without a clear understanding of the new covenant reality in which we now live.

We should always be careful to interpret the Old Testament, *through* the New Testament. By that I mean we should be rooted and grounded in our understanding of who we are in Christ and what the life, death and resurrection of Jesus really means to us today and has achieved for us in eternity - then I believe the Lord is able to breathe life and relevance and power into challenging texts like 2 Chronicles 7:14. We must understand that this verse is <u>not</u> a formula for revival - although thousands of sermons, books and songs seem to suggest that. It is just not that simple.

I devoted a lot of space early in this book dealing with some of the 'if …then' realities of life and how so often God chooses not to act in certain ways until we fulfil our part of the partnership.

The Bible, all of Church history and even our own experience will tell us that there are certain things God *chooses* to not do until we act in a certain way. However, to take that the next step and say there are certain things God *can't* do until we act in a certain way … is to deny His sovereign power.

God choosing not to act because of us is very different to God being unable to act because of our actions or inaction.

A covenant … is not a contract.

A partnership … is not a clinical, cause-and-effect, business deal.

A relationship … is not an exact science.

A promise … is not a formula.

God says: *"If My people who are called by My name …"* He is talking about relationship. He is talking about intimacy, communion, unity of heart, mind and purpose. He is talking to those for whom Jesus died; those whose names are written in the Lamb's Book of Life; those whose tickets to heaven have been bought and paid for by none other than Jesus. And what does He say to these people? He says this:

> *"When you allow the life which I have placed in you to emerge …*
> *when you submit to the power within … when you let Christ*
> *Who is in you, the hope of glory … shine in and through your*
> *life … then you will see the fruit of that submission and*
> *surrender. You will see My Spirit move in your life, your family,*
> *your Church, your city and your entire nation!"*

That is the essence of this much-quoted verse. It's not a simple, mathematical formula for revival. In fact, there really is nothing 'simple' or 'mathematical' about humbling ourselves, praying, seeking God's face and turning from our sin!

I have devoted a large part of this book to exploring the depths of our responses to God and how they permeate everything we think, say, and do. These 'tasks' or 'responsibilities' which are presented here as our part in this partnership, can only be played out on the stage of relationship.

If we are in fact the *"my people"* God is referring to in this verse; if we are the people whom He has called into this wonderful partnership; if we are the people of God whom He desires to use to heal this land; then we must understand that His bidding is His enabling. He never calls us to be or to do that which He does not Himself empower us to be and to do.

⇒ *Christ is in us, the Hope of Glory.* (Col.1:27)

⇒ *It's no longer we who live, but Christ Who lives in us.* (Gal.3:20)

⇒ *It is God who works in us to will and to act according to His good purpose.* (Phil.2:13)

⇒ *The fruit of the Spirit of God is love, joy, peace, patience, kindness, gentleness, goodness and self-control.* (Gal.5:22)

⇒ *We are servants of the gospel by the gift of God's grace given to us through the working of his power.* (Eph. 3:7)

⇒ *God is able to do immeasurably more than all we ask or imagine, according to his power that is at work within us.* (Eph. 3:20)

⇒ *It is by His power that He fulfils every good purpose of ours and every act prompted by our faith.* (2 Thes.1:11)

Do we get the picture? On the one hand God calls us into partnership and tells us that we have an incredibly important role in His plan, purpose, and mission on earth. We are His key players. It says in Ephesians 3:10 that God's intent is that *"…through the Church (that's you and me!) the manifold wisdom of God should be made known to the rulers and authorities in the heavenly realms."*

He has no 'Plan B.' When God says He is going to heal our land, save His people and bring His lost children home, how is He going to do that? Through whom shall He work? He has no one else other than you and me and all those who claim to be His people in this city and this nation.

It is through us and only us that God will fulfil His purpose – not because He has no choice, but because that is His choice – to use us. Our responsibility in the transformation of our city and our nation is without question. God has high hopes for you and me. He plans for us to be revealing His manifold wisdom to even angels and demons (rulers and authorities in the heavenly realms).

So, let's be very clear about the role we have in the wider scheme of things. God has no intention of waving His sovereign hand across the nation, changing the minds and hearts of all people overnight. He is more than able to do just that. There is nothing at all stopping Him from doing it right now - other than His own will and purpose.

God's plan, as revealed so clearly to us in the Bible, is to work with us, His much-loved people, His children, His disciples, His soldiers in the army of God, as together, we march against the powers of darkness every day. Our responsibility is very clear and very important and that is because God has chosen it to be so. It's a hard road for Him, for we are sinful, weak, disobedient, and frail creatures. But God's deep passion for a relationship and a partnership; His passion to let us be part of His unbelievable cosmic plan, is what moves God to include us in this incredible global mission.

Our responsibility is very clear and most of us take it far too lightly. Deep down we might think (or hope) that God will just do whatever He wants one day, in spite of us. That is clearly not the case. The Bible, all of Church history and our own personal journey, testify that whilst God *can* do it that way, He chooses not to. Instead, He calls us to be part of His plan.

On the other hand, the flip side of this coin, the counterpart of our responsibility is the promise that God will be our strength and our power and our source of purpose and motivation. At first glance, and without a clear understanding of the rest of Scripture, this verse in 2 Chronicles 7:14 seems to imply that our first task is to humble ourselves, pray, seek His face, and turn from our sin and <u>then</u> God's task is to heal our land.

That narrow interpretation is what gives us a formula, not a promise. The fact is, God is active from beginning to end in this process, and in our lives. Without the presence and power of God in our daily lives; without His amazing grace (His empowering presence) at work in us; we cannot begin to know what it means to humble ourselves, pray, seek His face, or turn from our sin.

> *"But by the grace of God I am what I am, and his grace to me was not without effect. No, I worked harder than all of them - yet not I, but the grace of God that was with me." (1 Corinthians 15:10)*

> *"In Him we have redemption through his blood, the forgiveness of sins, in accordance with the riches of God's grace that he lavished on us with all wisdom and understanding. And he made known to us the mystery of his will according to his good pleasure, which he purposed in Christ ... " (Ephesians 1:7-9)*

> *"My grace is sufficient for you, for my power is made perfect in weakness. Therefore, I will boast all the more gladly about my weaknesses, so that Christ's power may rest on me. That is why, for Christ's sake, I delight in weaknesses, in insults, in hardships, in persecutions, in difficulties. For when I am weak, then I am strong." (2 Corinthians 12:9-10)*

Thousands of years before any of those wonderful verses were written, a man called Zechariah gave us an even clearer message which is universally applicable in days of old and today:

> *"It's not by might nor by power, but by my Spirit,' says the LORD Almighty." (Zechariah 4:6)*

The Spirit of the living God; the presence of God within us; His empowering presence; His grace; is what will enable us to fulfil our calling and purpose. Many years after Zechariah's scrolls were laid to rest, the Apostle Paul spoke of the Spirit of God also. Study these familiar words and may God breath fresh life and power into them as you read them.

> *"We do, however, speak a message of wisdom among the mature, but not the wisdom of this age or of the rulers of this age, who are coming to nothing. No, we speak of God's secret wisdom, a wisdom that has been hidden and that God destined for our glory before time began. None of the rulers of this age understood it, for if they had, they would not have crucified the Lord of glory. However, as it is written: "No eye has seen, no ear has heard, no mind has conceived what God has prepared for those who love him" - but God has revealed it to us by his Spirit."*

> *"The Spirit searches all things, even the deep things of God. For who among men knows the thoughts of a man except the man's spirit within him? In the same way no one knows the thoughts of God except the Spirit of God. We have not received the spirit of the world but the Spirit who is from God, that we may understand what God has freely given us. This is what we speak, not in words taught us by human wisdom but in words taught by the Spirit, expressing spiritual truths in spiritual words."*

> *"The man without the Spirit does not accept the things that come from the Spirit of God, for they are foolishness to him, and he cannot understand them, because they are spiritually discerned. The spiritual man makes judgments about all things, but he himself is not subject to any man's judgment: "For who has known the mind of the Lord that he may instruct him?" But we have the mind of Christ." (1 Corinthians 2:6-16)*

Brothers and sisters, God wants to heal our land. God wants to heal every land across the world. He wants the light of His righteousness, ruth and justice to overpower the darkness of sin, deception and oppression.

He wants all of His lost, rebellious prodigals to come home and be embraced by His strong, loving arms of grace. He wants us to want that as much as He wants that. God wants our hearts to break over our city, our nation, and our world - just like His heart is breaking every day. Even more than that, God is going to use anything and everything at His disposal to bring us, His people, to that point of humility, prayer, intimacy, and repentance, so that His power can be unleashed in us.

This is why in every place around the world where God is now moving with unprecedented power and effectiveness, the reality of 2 Chronicles 7:14 is being played out in daily people's lives. Humility, prayer, brokenness, repentance, and intimacy with God are all vital components of every revival.

The question people have debated for centuries is a 'chicken and egg' dilemma. Which comes first – the Sovereign move of God to bring humility, prayer and repentance in His people ... OR ... is it the decision of His people to humble themselves, pray, seek His face and turn from their sin which 'triggers' or 'activates' or 'releases' the power of God in our midst to bring revival and heal our land?

Our western mindset can be a blessing sometimes and at other times it can be a curse. All too often we take a "both/and" reality and turn it into an "either/or" reality. That is what many people have done with this question of revival. The Sovereignty of God and the responsibility of man should never be set against each other as adversaries, alternate viewpoints or opposing sides to an argument. The Arminian - Calvinist debates centuries ago were by and large a total waste of time and a tragic testimony to our inability to hold two equally valid truths in tension together as the Bible does.

Like two sides to a coin or two perfectly parallel railway tracks, God's sovereignty and omnipotence stands unquestioned – right alongside our personal responsibility to make choices which are consistent with His purpose and will in order to see the fruit of those choices impact our lives and the lives of others.

So, in reference to revival and the age-old question: which comes first, our actions or the sovereign move of God's spirit - the answer is so clear in the Bible and in church history, that I cannot understand why so much debate has ensued.

The answer is <u>both</u>. They are as inseparable as two sides of a coin. They are as essential in the process of God healing our land as the left and right railway track. If we try to stress one at the expense of the other, the train is derailed, and much damage is done.

2 Chronicles 7:14 seems to imply that our first priority is to humble ourselves and I addressed that early in this book when I said that humility is the 'key to the Throne Room of God.' I spent a lot of time dealing with humility and pride. However, I would suggest that humbling ourselves is not possible unless we allow the Spirit of God to empower that intention and make it possible.

This verse has been used in millions of churches, books, sermons and songs as the 'foundational' verse for revival … if not for the whole purpose of the Church. Well, if it is that simple, why are we not all in revival right now?

I want to offer you a different foundational verse now - one which, if accepted and followed, will breathe life and power into 2 Chronicles 7:14 and every other promise in the whole Bible. It is not a verse you might expect, but it is one I believe carries the secret to all others.

> *"Whom have I in heaven but you? And earth has nothing*
> *I desire besides you." (Psalm 73:25)*

We end this book where we began. The first chapter was called *"A Hard Word'* and I talked about desire and how foundational it is to everything God wants to do in us and through us. *"Earth has nothing I desire besides you."*

Until we get to the place of saying that and believing that, then 2 Chronicles 7:14 will carry no secrets, no power and it will bear no fruit.

Until everyone and everything in our lives stands second to God; until knowing Him, loving Him, being near to Him, becomes our deepest desire, our greatest pleasure and primary motivation for living; we will continue to thrash around in a mire of mediocrity; singing about revival, praying for revival, longing to be part of revival in our land, yet still not becoming the channel and conduit for that revival.

God is not going to revive and heal the land through anyone other than His people. God has nobody other than you and me through whom He can channel His nation-transforming power. So, as we finish this journey together here, I plead with you to hear the Father's voice today:

"If My people will seek me while I may be found, call on Me while I am near; draw near to me; seek first My Kingdom and my righteousness; wait upon me and renew their strength … then they will soar on wings like eagles; they will run and not grow weary, they will walk and not be faint; and I will heal their land, because, My people will find me, when they seek me with all their heart."